CAREERS IN PRO SPORTS

CAREERS IN PRO SPORTS

by
Cordner Nelson

THE ROSEN PUBLISHING GROUP, Inc.
New York

Published in 1990 by The Rosen Publishing Group, Inc.
29 East 21st Street, New York, NY 10010

Copyright 1990 by Cordner Nelson

First Edition

Library of Congress Cataloging-In-Publication Data

Nelson, Cordner.
  Careers in pro sports / by Cordner Nelson.—
  1st ed.
    p.   cm.
  Includes bibliographical references.
  Summary: Looks at careers in professional
sports—the possibilities, life, training, and salaries,
as well as alternative careers to actually playing.
  ISBN 0-8239-1027-X
  1. Sports—Vocational guidance—United States—
Juvenile literature. [1. Sports—Vocational guid-
ance. 2. Vocational guidance.] I. Title.
GV583.N36   1989   89-37641
                                          CIP
                                           AC

Manufactured in the United States of America

About the Author

Cordner Nelson studied to be a coach, but World War II disrupted his plans. Instead, he became founding editor of *Track & Field News* in 1948 and subsequently was elected to the Track and Field Hall of Fame as a journalist rather than as athlete or coach.

Nelson is the author of a sports novel, *The Miler*, and one of the few best sellers about track, *The Jim Ryun Story*. He has also written two other biographical books, *Track & Field: The Great Ones* and *Track's Greatest Champions*. His 1973 history *Runners and Races: 1500/Mile* was updated twelve years later to *The Milers*. He is the author of two books on training, *The Advanced Running Book* for middle- and long-distance runners and *Excelling in Sports/How to Train* for all sports. Most recently he has written articles on track and field for two encyclopedias, *World Book* and *Americana*.

Nelson says, "I know what I'm writing about from sad experience when I advise young athletes to follow their natural abilities rather than their emotions. My emotions directed me to be a distance runner, but my ability won few races. I should have put all that effort into golf or tennis or some other accuracy sport. I think this is the most important advice in this book: Don't be as dumb as I was."

To David

Contents

Chapter I

The Benefits of Pro Sports

Here is one of the most valuable secrets for a good life: Earn your living doing something you like so much you would do it for nothing.

Millions of young people compete in sports for the sheer joy of it, and thousands make a career of sports. They enjoy their work and gain additional benefits while many of them become rich and famous.

A career in professional sports offers some dazzling enticements. If you can make the grade. . .

You can become a millionaire while playing a game you would play for fun.

You can become a celebrity, familiar to the millions of sports fans who watch in stadiums and on television.

Your work time will be much shorter than in regular jobs.

Your chances for a healthier life will be greatly improved because of the exercise and the professional care you give your body.

Your influence on other people, because of your fame and contacts, will give you more opportunities to do good in the world. President Franklin D. Roosevelt said, "Sport is the very fiber of all we stand for. It keeps our spirits alive."

Your fame and contacts will also boost your opportunities in future nonplaying jobs in or out of sports.

Children begin participating in sports for more than one reason, but the most popular reason is fun. They enjoy games, especially active games, and they play street stickball or sandlot baseball, touch football, pickup basketball, schoolyard soccer; when they have the opportunity they try tennis, golf, bowling, hockey, and racquetball. They like to be active, burning off excess energy, and they enjoy social contact with others. Sportswriter Jimmy Cannon wrote, "Sports is the toy department of life." After this casual beginning, some of them discover that they like to compete, and they add a layer of competitiveness on top of their enjoyment of simply playing. The desire to prove themselves good at something is a powerful driving force.

Other motives increase sports participation. Parents encourage sports for the beneficial exercise. Other parents push their children toward excellence to boost their own egos. Boys often choose football to impress girls. High school students who are good in a sport may work at it to win a scholarship to college. Few young beginners have the motive of becoming rich and famous as a professional athlete. Thus, you can begin sports for the best of reasons and enjoy whatever you play. Later, if you find yourself to be exceptionally good, you can begin to think of a career in pro sports.

Your chances of earning a lot of money are better in pro sports than in almost anything else. The huge sums of money paid to athletes increase each year and not only because of inflation. Sports continue to grow in popularity, which results in record gate receipts. Even more significant is the interest of television. When you read that NBC will pay $401 million for the rights to telecast the 1992 Olympic Games to the United States, you know that Americans want to watch sports. And where television is concerned, such interest means money. Much of this extra money trickles down to the athletes, and recent bargaining has resulted in a larger share for them.

Huge amounts of money also pour into sports from American businesses trying to cash in with advertising. Corporations were to spend $1.5 billion in 1989 on sports events bearing their name, according to *Special Events Report*, and endorsements by athletes were expected to total $100 million.

Sport magazine publishes its SPORT 100 each year, listing the 100 highest paid athletes. Its first survey, in 1983, showed 23 athletes earning a million dollars or more that year. That total rose to 37 in 1984, 46 in 1985, 88 in 1986, and 118 in 1987. Sports has become a gold mine, or rather several gold mines, and the inflation is expected to continue.

To understand the fabulous richness of this gold mine you should have in mind the annual salaries of other Americans. Here are some 1988 income figures for various occupations:

President of the United States	$200,000
Associate justice, Supreme Court	110,000
Four-star general	90,705
Member of Congress	89,500
Average starting salary, engineer	29,820
U.S. median family income, 1986	29,460
Average manufacturing job	21,714
52 x 40-hour weeks @ $3.35 per hour	6,968

And here are some income figures for various sports:

BOXING: Nothing in sports or anywhere else compares with Mike Tyson's $21 million purse for 1 minute 31 seconds of boxing in 1988. Michael Spinks, knocked out by Tyson, received $13.5 million! Larry Holmes was paid $6,625,000 in 1986, while both Marvin Hagler and Thomas Hearns collected $5 million each. In 1987 Hagler was paid $15 million for a fight he lost to Sugar Ray Leonard, who received $10.8 million. Tyson picked up $6.6 million for four fights in 1987. Muhammad Ali is the biggest money winner of all time in all sports, collecting about $62 million during his long career.

BASEBALL: More money is paid to major-league baseball players than to the players of any other sport. In 1988 the average salary of the 650 major leaguers, according to the Major League Baseball Players Association, was $438,729. In 1987 ten players were paid at least $2 million.

Stated another way, the average major leaguer, in his five-year career, earns twice as much money as the average worker earns in a lifetime.

FOOTBALL: In 1986 Steve Young, then of the Tampa Bay Buccaneers, was credited with an income of more than $3 million.

BASKETBALL: With only 276 players in the National Basketball Association, it is the most exclusive of all sports. The minimum salary is $100,000, and the average is around $600,000.

HOCKEY: No hockey players made the SPORT 100, but Wayne Gretzky, probably the greatest of all time, was paid $948,000 before his trade to the Los Angeles Kings in 1988. Ten players were paid $425,000 or more in 1987.

TENNIS: Martina Navratilova had career earnings of $13,341,712 by mid-1988, while Ivan Lendl had won $12,648,060. John McEnroe, whose behavior would see him fired from many jobs, was approaching the $10 million mark. Lendl won over $2 million in 1987, and three other men won more than a million. Steffi Graf won $1,063, 785 that year, and four other women won more than $600,000.

GOLF: Ian Woosnam of Wales won $1,793,268 in 1987, including an even million for one South African victory. In 1988 Curtis Strange led the U.S. tour with a record $1,147,644, and 112 men won over $100,000. Many of them won more money in Europe or Japan. Leading money winner among women on the LPGA tour for 1988 was Sherri Turner with $360,851, and 70 women won more than $36,000. Seniors, golfers over fifty, now play for far more money than when they were in their prime. Leader for 1988 was Bob Charles with $533,929, while 24 others won more than $129,000.

BOWLING: Mike Aulby set a single-season record in the new PBA in 1986 by winning $201,200. Pete Weber led in 1987 with $179,516, and four others topped $140,000. The Professional Bowling Association pays out about $4 million in prize money.

HORSE RACING: Four jockeys collected more than a million dollars each in 1986 and 1987, with Laffit Pincay Jr. on top with $1,341,505 in 1986. Willie Shoemaker, in his mid-fifties, won about $700,000 in both 1986 and 1987.

HARNESS RACING: Bill Haughton received about 10

percent of the $40.2 million in purses he won in his 43-year career.

RODEO: Five rodeo riders won over $100,000 in 1986 and 1987. Lewis Feild led with $144,335 in 1987.

TRACK: Still in transition between amateurism and professionalism, track has few offical winnings. Most track income is from contracts with sponsors, endorsements, and appearance money. SPORT guessed at these earnings for 1986: Carl Lewis $800,000, Mary Slaney $550,000, Edwin Moses $500,000, Steve Jones $450,000, and Carlos Lopes $450,000. Lewis is said to have turned down $80,000 for one race in Italy when he preferred to go home, and he and Ben Johnson were paid $250,000 each for one race in 1988. Russia announced payments of more than $24,000 for each gold medal won in the 1988 Olympics. Reports say Florence Joyner-Griffith has accumulated more than $1 million for her sensational Olympic year.

RACQUETBALL: Marty Hogan made about half a million a year in the 1980's.

AUTO RACING: Dale Earnhardt earned $1,699,621 m 1987.

SPORT also listed some winnings in odd sports. Lonnie Stanley made $111,661 for freshwater bass fishing, and Rhonda Wilcox led the women with $41,550. Mike Hazelwood won $38,850 in water skiing, and Deena Brush won $52,325. Table tennis paid little, with top winner Dan Seemiller collecting only $3,415.

Nonplayers also earn large salaries. Football coach Bill Walsh retired after a $1.3 million income in 1988, and announcer Brent Musburger was paid $1.9 million in 1986.

The most money is paid by corporations in advertising. They pay huge sums to well-known athletes or former athletes who will endorse their products. For the single year of 1987, *Sports Marketing Newsletter* estimated these earnings from endorsements:

Arnold Palmer (golf)	$8,000,000
Jack Nicklaus (golf)	6,000,000

Boris Becker (tennis)	6,000,000
Greg Norman (golf)	4,500,000
Michael Jordan (basketball)	4,000,000
Ivan Lendl (tennis)	3,000,000
John Madden (former football coach)	3,000,000
Jim McMahon (football)	3,000,000
Dennis Connor (yachting)	2,000,000
Chris Evert (tennis)	2,000,000
Martina Navratilova (tennis)	2,000,000
Jackie Stewart (retired race car driver)	2,000,000

The fame that comes to sports heroes brings with it the possibility of more money, the mental comfort of confidence in yourself, and something like thousands of instant "friends." If you have been a famous athlete, many people will recognize you and want to talk with you. After a World Series or Super Bowl the stars are usually interviewed on television talk shows, and many are even invited to the White House. Fame brings offers of various ways to earn more money and makes it easier for the ex-athlete to get a job or enter business. Many stars own restaurants or sporting goods stores where people spend money in hopes of seeing the athlete.

Fourteen years after he retired from baseball, Mickey Mantle said, "I get more fan mail now than I ever did. I get letters now that almost make you cry. They tell me that looking up to me gave them inspiration to become what they are."

As a professional athlete you will have more free time than in most other jobs. Your working days are shorter, and you will have an off season of three to six months. Several pros have gone through medical school in their spare time while earning large salaries. Chi Chi Rodriguez said of Jack Nicklaus, "He's the only golfer in history who has become a living legend in his spare time."

You will have time to study for a career in business, the media, or almost any profession. Where else can you earn enough to retire, study for any vocation, and give yourself the name recognition that will open doors to that vocation—all at the same time?

You will benefit from better health. You cannot be successful as an athlete if you have poor health, so part of your effort will go into learning to protect and improve your body. Long ago Benjamin Franklin said, "Games lubricate the body and the mind," and today the benefits of exercise are becoming widely known.

For anybody who loves to play and is good enough for the pros, it would be difficult to find a better job.

Chapter II

The Disadvantages of Pro Sports

Now for the bad news. If you think pro sports offer you a glamorous life full of wealth, fame, and fun you are right, but you have heard only one side of the story. A career in pro sports also offers you disillusionment, heartbreak, and failure. Before you go much farther you should take a realistic look at the dark side.

Disadvantage #1—Tough Competition

The very same rewards that make a sports career so desirable also put it out of reach of most athletes. Millions of young athletes dream of the glamorous life, but there is room for only a few to succeed. Consider some statistics:

Only 1,372 positions are open in the National Football League. Thus, a high school player must be better than one in a thousand to have a chance at professional football. Basketball is even more difficult, with only 276 NBA jobs. There are only 650 major league baseball players. Golf has a little over 200 on tour.

Former pro footballer Norm Van Brocklin said, "There's no tougher way to make easy money than pro football."

Disadvantages #2—Injuries

In some sports, notably football, the possibility of injury is a constant threat. Before each week's games the NFL releases a list of dozens of players who are injured. Some of them play anyway, although not always at their best. A few are out for the season. An outstanding player is kept under contract while missing a whole season, but more often his career ends without a chance to show his true worth.

No figures are available as to how many players are lost because of injuries. Beginning in high school, many players drop out because of injuries and more drop out of college sports. Of the 5.8 million high school athletes, an estimated one million are injured each year. It is no fun to play a game if you are injured time after time. What's worse, your chances of gaining a college scholarship or a pro contract are much less if you are injury-prone.

Sports medicine authorities say that a certain amount of brain injury is inevitable in boxing, football, and soccer.

Roger Craig, the great running back for the San Francisco 49 ers, suffers much wear and tear in a game. He says, "After a game I look like I've been locked in a cage with a tiger." He has imprints of face masks on his back, gouges from turf burns on his arms, and bruises from cleats on his hands. "I can sense there's internal bleeding from all the blows and bruises because for several hours my body temperature is very warm. I can't eat that night, and I have difficulty sleeping."

Richard Todd, quarterback for the New York Jets, tells about a 1981 game: "I don't know if I should tell you this, but I was injected six times in my front and five times in my back just prior to that game. Then at halftime I got shot up in the ribs and the cartilage again."

Dr. James Parker, team physician for the New York Mets, says, "Every time a man pitches, he is systematically injuring his arm. A pitcher's durability will depend on the genetic capacity of the arm to recover from the insult of pitching."

In the 1970s the Canadian Ophthalmological Society found thirty-seven Canadian pro hockey players who were blind in one eye from playing injuries.

If you have more than your share of injuries, give serious consideration to specializing in a different sport.

Disadvantage #3—Lack of Freedom

Even if you break into a pro sport, your contract binds you to one team for a number of years. If you do not like the coach or he does not like you, chances are that you will sit on the bench more than you like. If you do not like the city that is your new home, you cannot change it. You may have to put up with a situation you dislike for five years before you have any freedom of choice.

Your team can cut you or trade you to another team, and you have no rights at all. You may have a team owner like George Steinbrenner of the New York Yankees who will criticize you unfairly in public, but you have no choice but to do as you are told until you have been there enough years to become a free agent. You may have to play while injured, with a risk to your future career.

If you are a superstar and get along with everybody, none of this will happen, but a large number of professional athletes suffer from a lack of freedom.

Tennis champion Billy Jean King said this of her successor, Chris Evert: "Chris is riding the crest of a wave, and I hope she enjoys it. It's the best time of her life. But I also pity her; she hasn't a free moment to herself. Chris no longer belongs to Chris Evert. She belongs to the public."

Disadvantage #4—Life on the Road

People who have never been away from home tend to glamorize travel more than do people who travel. After a game, sometimes near midnight, players have to ride a bus to an airport, wait for their plane, fly for up to five hours, then ride another bus to a hotel. It is not a restful night.

Major-league baseball players do this about thirty times each season. Basketball players travel even more, but football players travel to only eight away games plus a few exhibition games. Golfers travel as much as baseball players, and tennis players travel most of all.

If you do not like to fly, or if you cannot sleep on a plane, these trips can feel like a real hardship. Add the lack of regular hours for sleeping, a poor choice of food, and few hours of free time and you have a life you would not choose.

Disadvantage #5—Wrong Life-Style

It is natural for creatures, human or animal, to reform themselves into their environment. The environment of young, energetic athletes, given sudden wealth and separated from the good influence of hometown and family, tends to lead many of them astray.

Peter Gent, a former football pro who wrote *North Dallas Forty*, said, "Athletes hang around with people who tell them, 'The rules don't apply to you.'" Don Reese confessed in a *Sports Illustrated* article in 1982: "Cocaine arrived in my life with my first-round draft into the NFL in 1974. It has dominated my life.... Eventually, it took control and almost killed me....Cocaine may be found in quantity throughout the NFL. It's pushed on players....Sometimes it's pushed *by* players ....Just as it controlled me, it now controls and corrupts the game, because so many players are on it."

Another loss is often the joys of a young family. Professional athletes are away from home almost as much as sailors. If you are married, it becomes a hardship for both you and your spouse. If you have children, it is hard on them and lonely for you.

Disadvantage #6—Loss of Desire to Play

For one reason or another your sport can turn into drudgery instead of fun.

A game you played for fun can become a job where you are continually looking over your shoulder at somebody who wants to take it away from you. In college if you go into a slump for a while the worst that can happen to you is some bench time. As a pro you might lose your job and not find another. For some athletes that means constant fear, and fear can take the joy out of playing. Or you might simply outgrow your sport. Your values change as you grow older, and you might find some activity you would rather do. Or, as with many other activities, too much of a good thing may simply wear out your enjoyment of it.

Roger Maris of the Yankees hit sixty-one homers in 1961, and it left him a bitter man: "They did everything they could to downgrade them. They acted as though I was doing something wrong, poisoning the record books or something. Do you know what I have to show for the sixty-one home runs? Nothing. Exactly nothing."

Bernie Parent, former goalie for the Philadelphia Flyers, said, "There is a built-in discipline to playing any sport, a structure that keeps you within certain bounds. I played hockey for twenty-five years. All of a sudden, I couldn't play anymore. The discipline was gone."

If your game is no longer fun, you'll do it solely for the rewards—money and fame. The catch is, you won't do it as well and you will lose the rewards sooner.

Disadvantage #6—Loss of Desire to Play

You have heard of good players at the age of forty. If you continue to earn a large salary, and if you invest properly, you will not need to work for money for the rest of your life. But what are your chances of playing until you are forty? If you play at all—sign a contract—you will have, on the average, a career of less than five years! The average player in baseball, football, basketball, and hockey lasts less than five years.

A short career in itself is no reason to decide against trying, but the strong possibility means you should think hard about what else you will do with your life. For many pros, life after sports is a hard letdown. Fame evaporates rapidly, and suddenly you must adjust your self-esteem and take your place among the common people.

Disadvantage #8—Uncertain Income

Once you have signed a contract you know how much you will be paid for the duration of that contract. You do not know if you will ever receive another contract. And some contracts provide for termination if you do not perform as well as you both hope. In many sports your income is in the form of prize money. Golfers, tennis players, bowlers, rodeo riders all must perform well to have any income at all. They must win enough money to pay for their food and lodging and their travel expenses to the next tournament. It is said that a pro golfer must win at least $25,000 to pay for the minimum of expenses.

Disadvantage #9—Underdevelopment

The harder you work at becoming a great athlete, the more time and thought you devote to it, the less time and thought you will give to other activities. Your intellectual development will suffer. Other ambitions you may have will be delayed or canceled. It is possible to delay an important career until after your pro sports career, but it is much more difficult. Senator Bill Bradley did it, waiting to enter politics until after his basketball career ended; but he is an exceptional man, and politics does not require as much time and preparation as other professions. Many athletes are too content with their income and life-style, and they suffer from the loss of fame when their career is over.

Disadvantage #10—Stress

Psychiatrist Grigori Raiport says, "The professional athlete has more stress than the average person. Every third athlete suffers an adverse effect from stress. They are more stress-resistant than the average person but still, every third of them breaks down."

Fran Tarkenton, still a great quarterback at thirty-seven,

pointed out some of the stress: "Physically I'm sure I can play next year. The only question is, do I want to put up with all the crap? When you lose, you walk down the street and people come over and tell you, 'You're too old. Why don't you get the hell out?'"

These are definite disadvantages, but for most athletes they do not outweigh the strong attraction of a pro career. If you have the athletic ability and the necessary mental toughness and if you love your sport, then go for it. This is not a situation where you risk everything and surrender all other opportunities in life. Fortunately, a career in pro sports begins with amateur sports. You can enjoy sports through high school and college while you prepare for another career just as if you had never heard of professional sports. Then, if you are good enough and if you want to, you can decide to try for a professional career. You can have the best of both worlds!

Chapter III

Plan Your Career

If you decide to try for a career in professional sports you want to know how to go about it. You need some sort of plan to keep you headed in the right direction. A little thought in advance will save you a lot of wrong turns and headaches.

Before you make an outline of a tentative plan, you need to do a little thinking about what is involved. Think about these questions:

How Do You Become a Great Athlete?

Are great athletes born or made? The answer is—both. You need both great natural ability and the ideal environment to become a great athlete. Think about it this way. You were born with a certain amount of potential ability. Nothing you ever do will make you better than that potential. Everything you do after being born determines how close you come to reaching your potential.

To visualize this situation, start at the bottom of a piece of paper and draw a rectangle one inch wide. The height of the rectangle determines the total area. That is your potential. If your rectangle is only six inches high and somebody else has a rectangle ten inches high, you will be at a disadvantage. Now fill in your rectangle, starting from the bottom, to represent how much you have progressed toward your potential. If you accomplish the maximum progress, your rectangle will be full.

17

If the other athlete's rectangle is only half full, it will reach only five inches high while yours is six, and you will win.

You cannot do anything to improve the height of your rectangle, but you can take two equally important steps: (1) You can choose the sport in which your rectangle is high enough to give you a chance. (2) You can develop yourself so that your rectangle is almost full. If you find a sport in which your natural potential is adequate and if you work to reach that potential, you will become a good athlete.

One of the great secrets of sport is the fact that although you cannot increase the potential you were born with, you *can* do something about it. That is because you have several abilities and each sport requires different abilities. The secret then is to try the sport in which you have the greatest ability.

How to Exploit Your Natural Ability

You were born with certain natural attributes. Some of those must be much better than average if you hope to be a professional athlete. Luckily, one strong quality, intensely developed, is enough to turn you into a pro. Your main problem, the single most important decision you'll ever make with regard to playing a professional sport, is to select your best sport.

Nobody knows, of course, but it is undoubtedly true that thousands of potentially great athletes never play seriously at their best sport. There are probably hundreds of basketball players not quite good enough for the NBL who could have been ranked near the top in tennis. There are many marginal football players who could have been great in track and field. For every good professional player, there is probably someone with similar natural ability who never tried that sport.

Why such inefficiency? Many reasons: (1) People aim for the high-paying sports where the competition is much tougher. (2) People fall in love with a sport and devote all their time to it instead of to a sport in which they have more ability. (3) Some lack opportunity, such as inner-city kids who spend hours shooting baskets and never see a golf course nor belong to a tennis club. (4) Parents often direct their children to other goals, many of them outside of sports. (5) Many never develop their ability because they don't know it is there, or they have not learned to like that sport, or they are lazy, or they are in love.

One of the sadest stories in sports is the player who works extra hard under the wise direction of a good coach and yet never approaches greatness because he is in the wrong sport. Your most important obligation to yourself is to aim yourself in the right direction.

Pepper Martin of the St. Louis Cardinals once said, "You can take an ol' mule and run him and feed him and train him and get him in the best shape of his life, but you ain't going to win the Kentucky Derby."

The most common way to find your best sport is to try many to learn where your talents fit best. The main drawback is that it takes a year or two of playing and practicing to learn some of the skills, and so you have time for no more than a few sports. A better way is to think about your natural attributes and choose a few sports accordingly. Consider these:

- Your height. Surprisingly, few sports require greater than average height, although it is an advantage in some. If you are on the short side you should not fall in love with basketball unless you are one in a million as a long shooter and extremely fast and agile.
- Your weight. Even more surprisingly, your weight is less decisive than your height because you have more control over it. Football linemen must be large, but your natural weight plus a little added weight from strength training will do for almost all other sports.
- Your strength. Few sports require great natural strength. You can develop enough strength for all the others. Natural strength is necessary for a fastball pitcher, for football linemen, and for wrestling and boxing.
- Your speed. Running speed is about 90 percent natural. If you are slow of foot you cannot play half of the football

positions and you will not reach the top in baseball, basketball, or soccer.

- Your quickness. This may be the single most important ability in sports. Apart from running speed, quickness means how fast you can react and begin the correct movement. You must be quick to change directions in reaction to your opponent. You must have fast muscles to put speed into such diverse movements as a tennis serve, a golf swing, and a left hook. Only a few sports do not need quickness, notably billiards, bowling, marathon running, and the all-important short game in golf.
- Your agility. Quickness means that you can start fast and move fast once you start. Agility means that you can make the movements correctly. The two should go together. If you are especially agile, you can be a baseball shortstop, a basketball playmaker, a boxer, wrestler, or racquetball player. You can judge your agility in such sports by how fast you can learn such skills as juggling, typing, dancing, skating, or playing Ping Pong.
- Your accuracy. You need special natural ability—in addition to much practice—to be a good passer, pitcher, putter, shooter, or placekicker. You need it in the offensive part of soccer and hockey. You can test your accuracy easily by comparing yourself to others in your ability to hit targets with any kind of ball or with darts or even rocks.
- Your endurance. You can develop much endurance, but you need the basis of exceptional natural endurance to be good as a marathon runner, cyclist, boxer, or soccer player. It will make you better at basketball, hockey, football, and tennis. You can judge your natural endurance only by comparing yourself with others who have had the same amount of training. If you tire more quickly than average, avoid the endurance sports.
- Your cooperation. In team sports you must cooperate, sometimes at a sacrifice to your personal record. For example, in basketball, do you try to add to your point total by shooting an 18-footer, or do you pass to a team-

mate with an easier shot? Rick Barry, who once made nineteen assists in one game as a forward, said, "A lot of players don't know what it is to make a pass. It's not that they don't know how; it's just that they're not looking for anybody." If you have trouble cooperating, try an individual sport.

* Your desire. The "hungry" athlete wins—if all else is close to equal. Your enthusiasm for what you are doing, in sports or anything else, determines how hard you are willing to work, how much time you will work, and how efficiently you will work. If you have a passion for one activity you will probably work extra hours at it, and so you will not have those extra hours for anything else. Unfortunately, time is limited.

Unless you have extraordinary natural ability you will not be a great success in sports, or most activities, without this passion that drives you to work hard. Therefore, if your talents lie in one direction and your interests in another, you have a problem. You must choose between what you want and what you can have. Fortunately, you are likely to find the two are identical much of the time, but avoid the mistake of trying to be a square peg in a round hole.

Your Decision

You don't have to decide right away. The younger you are, the longer you can wait. But you should begin the process of narrowing down your choices. With the help of your parents, teachers, coaches, and friends you can begin to find your strengths and weaknesses. By the time you start high school you should narrow your sports down to about five, such as three team sports and two individual. That is not an inflexible rule, but you will find it difficult to keep up with more. It does not mean that you cannot change during high school. You might try another sport for fun and like it enough to add it. Or you might suddenly have the opportunity to try a new sport, such as if your parents join a tennis club. But you will probably have to drop another sport to make room for the new one.

By the time you reach your senior year of high school you should be thinking of college scholarships, and so you will select one or two sports. The others will be eliminated, perhaps forever, or relegated to a weekend or summer recreation.

For most of your school career, high school and college, you can compete in one or more sports just like any other school athlete. Near your senior year in college you can decide about trying for a professional career. If you do not, you will have had your fun and competition, with perhaps a scholarship and all the other benefits. Thus, you have everything to gain and almost nothing to lose. Go for it!

Maximize Your Potential

Once you have found your best sport you can reach your maximum of potential ability by using many parts of your environment. Your parents can help by providing you with opportunity, such as joining a golf club or driving you to the skating rink. Family support is almost a necessity for success in sports. Your coaches can aid you immeasurably by teaching you skills, by directing your conditioning, by giving you good advice, and by inspirational leadership. You can also be helped by other people, by good health habits, and by books and films. But by far the most important aid to your attempt to fill your maximum potential can be summed up with a single small word—

Try

Many potentially great athletes have the other environmental advantages, but many of them fall short because they do not try as hard as they can. Perhaps they were superstars in high school and college and they continue to believe that their 80 percent effort is all it takes. Some athletes have so much natural ability that they stop trying before they reach their potential. This phenomenon is most easily seen in track. A world record is thought of as the ultimate, and most athletes who break a world record think they have gone about as far as they can go. But if you think back to when Roger Bannister first ran a mile under four minutes or Parry O'Brien first put the shot over 60 feet, you will see that nobody thought more effort would lead to many miles under 3:50 and many shot puts over 70 feet.

Other successful athletes are lazy, content to be good without going all out to be their best. Many do not know all the different ways they can try in order to improve. Most try hard in some ways but neglect others. To be truly great, an athlete must try as hard as possible in every way he knows and then try to find other ways. Joe DiMaggio said, "No boy from a rich family ever made the big leagues."

You don't have to look far to find examples of success as a result of trying. Do you remember when you learned to ride a bicycle? You simply kept trying until, as if by magic, you learned to balance. Do you know how jugglers learn to keep seven objects in the air with their two hands? They do it by trying for thousands of hours. A pianist plays the piano several hours a day for many years. You may envy a pro basketball player who earns a few hundred thousand a year for his shooting ability. Do you have any idea how many thousands of shots he practiced?

Jim Ryun became an "overnight" sensation as a sixteen-year-old sophomore. Few people knew that he had run an average of twelve miles a day for the previous year through rain, snow, and Kansas heat until often he could not eat his dinner. He *tried* as few athletes have ever tried, before or since.

Johnny Bench won Rookie of the Year honors, and people thought he was just naturally great. They didn't know that his father was a catcher, and that Johnny decided he wanted to be a ball player when he was seven, and that his father drilled him by the hour in throwing from the crouch to each base and fielding bunts and pop fouls.

Wayne Gretzky, possibly the greatest of all hockey players, had a father who taught him to skate when he was two. He practiced hockey for hours, and at five he played against ten-year-olds. He became a pro at seventeen and is usually hockey's Most Valuable Player. Jimmy Connors started tennis lessons at four. Nancy Lopez won a golf tournament at nine. The list goes on and on. Trying makes it happen.

Steve Garvey, the National League's Most Valuable Player in 1974, said, "The harder we work, the more it becomes a habit, and we learn that hard work turns into success."

If You Don't Play, What Else Can You Do?

If you love sports but lack the natural ability to be a professional athlete, or if you don't want to try, you can go into one of the many nonplaying jobs in sports.

Most of the fame and fortune from pro sports go to the athletes, but there are more jobs related to sports for non-players. Many athletes, whether or not they are good enough for the glamour jobs, go on to lifetime jobs in the sports they love. Here are some sports-related jobs you might consider:

Coaching. Every team, from high school to the pros, has one or more coaches. In any given year in the United States no more than about 5,000 professional athletes make a living as players, but there are more than 160,000 coaches. A coach must be an expert at the sport and a good leader.

Trainers. Although fewer in number than coaches, trainers have more secure jobs with far less stress. Trainers must learn as much as a doctor about sports injuries.

Sportswriters. Each newspaper usually has one to several full- or part-time sportswriters, and there are about 10,000 newspapers. Sportswriters usually know and love several sports.

Administrators. Sports need people to smooth the path, all the way from the commissioners of football and baseball down to the people who distribute tickets. Athletic directors are the best-known administrators, but there are many others.

Announcers. Radio and television announcers are a prominent part of sports because more people listen to sports than go
to the stadium. Only a relatively few jobs are available.

Make Your Plan

At this point you can begin making a general plan for your
sports career. You can use a loose-leaf notebook, adding and
changing goals as you go along. You can use the same notebook to keep a record of your progress in training and competition.

To begin with, your general plan should look something like
this:

1. Decide which sports to try. (Chapter III)
2. Begin playing.
3. Learn to study so you'll be eligible for school sports.
4. Learn how to train. (Chapter IV)
5. Learn how to compete. (Chapter V)
6. Manage your amateur career. (Chapter VI).
7. Decide whether to try to be a pro. If not, go to 10.
8. Work at breaking in as a pro. (Chapter VII)
9. Manage your professional career. (Chapter VIII)
10. Consider a sports-related career. (Chapter IX)

Chapter IV

Reach Your Potential Through Training

After you have considered your natural abilities and selected a sport, you need a training plan to help you reach your potential. Training can be divided into conditioning your body and learning skills. Before you can make plans you need to know the basics of how to condition your body and learn skills.

Conditioning

Conditioning involves improving your strength, speed, quickness, and endurance.

Before you consider each of those areas of improvement, you should think about how your body changes.

Your body changes as a response to stimuli. A stimulus is anything that causes a reaction, such as the burning pain from a hot stove or a 10-mile run.

Training is the proper selection of stimuli. You stimulate your body so that it will change. There are different kinds of stimuli, but the kind you need to *condition* your body is stress.

Stress is caused by any stimulus that disturbs your body. When stressed, your body fights back to protect itself, and if the stress continues your body's resistance causes permanent changes in your body. The most common example may be friction to your skin. Your body's reaction builds a callus to protect your skin.

The art and science of training consists of selecting stresses strong enough to cause your body to improve and yet not so strong as to harm your body. You can monitor your improvement easily. It is not so easy to be sure that you do not overtrain, even though there are many warning signs. Some of the symptoms of overtraining are fatigue, loss of enthusiasm, aches, weight loss, increased pulse rate, and decreases in your red corpuscle count and your hemoglobin values. One of the most valuable training secrets is the fact that you cannot recover fully in twenty-four hours. Most athletes now alternate hard days with easier days to avoid overtraining.

You can improve greatly if you increase stress gradually and avoid exhausting all of your adaptive energy.

The main benefits of training will be to your strength, your speed, your endurance, and your skills. Let's examine each of these, along with training efficiency.

Strength

You can be better at almost any sport by increasing your strength. Some sports, such as football, require great all-round strength. Other sports require strength in certain muscles, such as a pitcher's arm, a kicker's leg, or the muscles a batter uses to swing a bat.

A strong muscle means more speed because it can move your body faster. A strong muscle means more endurance because it needs less energy to do the same work. Almost any athlete can benefit from increased all-round strength because of increased speed and endurance.

It may help you to know a little about how muscles work. Each muscle is made up of thousands of muscle fibers in groups of 100 to 150. Each group is activated by a single motor nerve. The more power you want, the more groups are activated. For example, to hold an egg in your hand you would activate only one group. If you used all the groups you would crush the egg. When you use your muscles they become larger and stronger because each individual fiber thickens.

You can use five different methods for strength training. The easiest is *exercises* that use your body weight for resistance, such as pushups, pullups, and situps. These are limited in the amount of strength they can build.

Isometric contractions take place when you exert your muscular power against an immovable object. Unlike exercises in which resistance is your body weight or less, isometric exercises strain your muscles to the limit. But your muscles do not move, so you can strengthen only part of each muscle.

Resistance training is designed to allow movement of your muscles similar to the skill you use. Examples are the football charging sled, sprinting up a hill, and swinging a leaded bat. You can increase your strength, but you must be careful not to overdo the resistance for fear of ruining your form.

Weight training will develop more strength and do it faster. You should not start any heavy weight training without instruction from a competent coach, because some exercises are far better for you than others, and because you need to know the correct methods and safety precautions.

Circuit training is a series of exercises made up of any of the first four types. Arrange the exercises so that you can rest one part of your body while exercising another. Circuit training can also combine flexibility exercises, especially valuable because you need to follow each resistance movement with a natural movement so as to retain your correct form.

Before starting your strength program, you should have some sort of plan. Which muscles do you want to strengthen and by how much? Most athletes begin with general strengthening and add whatever specific strength they need for their sport.

Another question to answer as part of your planning: How much body weight do you want to add? If you are a football player, a heavyweight boxer, a shot-putter, or a skinny basketball player, you probably want to add weight. If you are a marathon runner, a jockey, a soccer player, a tennis player, or a weight-class boxer, you do not want to add weight. To avoid weight gain you should use lighter weights with more repetitions and do only a minimum of general strength training.

Next you need to understand how to strengthen a muscle. Your muscle fibers grow thicker and thus stronger through a chemical reaction to the stimulus of exhaustion. Therefore, the fastest and surest way to improve your strength is to exhaust your muscles. You should select a weight you can lift about eight or ten times but not more than about fifteen times. One such set is enough each day, and you should rest for about forty-eight hours between sessions to give your fibers time to grow.

One drawback to weight training is the equipment necessary. You need access to an elaborate set of "iron" or an expensive weight machine. If you want to work at it, you can substitute wall pulleys, weighted containers, or a rope wrapped around a bar to provide controlled resistance.

If you insist on beginning without a coach, you must at least read a book. You must know the safety rules and proper technique. You also need advice on your choice of lifts. Do not use the competitive weight-lifting exercises because they are more dangerous and less valuable. You should probably start with exercises such as the clean and press, abdominal curls, the bouncing split squat, and various arm exercises with dumbbells. Then add any exercise specific to your sport. As an example, a kicker wants to strengthen the muscles that flex the hip and extend the lower leg.

Circuit training is probably best for anybody, even if your only strength work is weight training. Stretch every muscle after strengthening it, and alternate the use of various parts of your body so that your legs rest while you work on your arms. And add a minute or so of "rest" while you go through the motions of your sport with no weight resistance so as to maintain your skills. Twice a week is enough weight training for maintaining strength, but you might do more for greater strength or for endurance training.

It is not at all uncommon for an athlete to increase the strength of certain muscle groups by more than 200 percent. You can improve almost any aspect of any sport through proper weight training. On the other hand, it is possible to decrease your skills through incorrect weight training, as Johnny Miller learned when his strengthened shoulder muscles ruined the rhythm of his great golf swing. Find some help and do it right.

Speed and Quickness

Running speed is of great value in many sports. Even a football lineman has more chance at a pro contract if his speed over forty yards is faster than average. Quickness is speed of movement, not necessarily in running. A basketball player without quickness had better be close to seven feet tall, and a slow boxer had better have the strength of a grizzly bear in his arms.

Speed and quickness are natural talents. Some people are born faster than others. Most people could never learn to run fast enough to be a sprinter or a halfback, and how many people are quick enough to be a pro basketball forward or a hockey goalie? You cannot improve your speed greatly, nothing like the 300 percent possible in strength training, but you can improve 10 percent. That is one yard in ten, enough to avoid a tackle or to be safe at first instead of out.

Even more impressive is the fact that the speed and quickness of your start and pickup can be improved the most, so that most athletes can improve 20 percent in the first few yards. Imagine how valuable it is to be two steps farther along in football, baseball, basketball, soccer, or tennis.

The best way to learn to run faster is to go out for track and learn from a professional coach. If you cannot do that and want to learn by yourself, it is not a simple process. You can run faster by increasing your leg speed, increasing the length of your stride, or both. This can be done by improving your sprinting skill and strengthening your running muscles.

The best example of the value of strength to a sprinter is Ben Johnson of Canada, who ran the two fastest 100s ever run. He spent more time than any other sprinter on weight training and enhanced it with steroids, for which he was disqualified from the 1988 Olympic Games. He looked more like a football player than a track man, but his speed was unsurpassed.

Added strength means that you can push your body farther along with each stride, thus a longer stride. It means that you can push your body faster, thus greater leg speed. It also means that you can lift your knees faster and higher and drive your feet down at the track faster and harder. The right kind of strength adds to your speed.

A considerable amount of skill is involved in running fast. Correct running form will make you faster. The most important part of your sprinting form is the length of your stride. A shorter stride is quicker, but a longer stride covers more ground, obviously. If you lengthen your stride it takes more time. Your goal is to find the optimum length for your stride by experimentation. You can check your speed by how it feels to you, by being timed, or, best, by how you gain or lose alongside another sprinter maintaining a steady sprint.

Other parts of the sprinting skill include high knee action, hip flexibility, elimination of waste movement, and relaxation. If you can move your legs fast and hard while relaxing all unneeded muscles, you will not only run faster but you will save strength for your next sprint.

To be a good sprinter you also need a fast start and pickup. The shorter the race, the more important these become, so the start and pickup are vital in sports requiring a short burst of speed.

Actually, a good start requires an advantageous starting position, a quick reflex, and correct form. A sprinter is allowed to use any starting position, and the sprint start has proved to be the fastest. The sprinter's hands are on the track with one foot farther back than the other. After a push with both feet and a step with the back foot, the sprinter's body is leaning far forward and all the power goes forward. If you used that power while standing upright, you would fall flat on your back. Therefore, in sports where you do not have time to take the optimum starting position you should approach it as closely as possible. A basketball or tennis player should be in a crouch rather than standing at attention. A baseball batter should learn to finish a swing with knees bent and body leaning toward first base.

A reflex action is more complicated than the usual example of jerking your hand away from a hot stove. You have to learn to react to a stimulus without conscious thought. A sprinter trains with a starting pistol until the sound is not delayed by any brain action. Nerve pathways change so that the sound of the gun seems to go directly to the legs. A basketball player must learn to react to something more complicated, such as an opponent's pass or even a movement of a foot.

The speed of your reflex is not as important as its correctness. You might have the fastest reaction on the basketball court, but if you step in the wrong direction you are two steps behind. The most important part of starting is making the correct movement. Thus, starting is a skill requiring practice until you master it. Few things are as important in the quickness sports such as tennis, basketball, boxing, hockey, and soccer. Think through your movements in slow motion, and work out the correct starting position and foot and arm movements. Then drill on them until they become a reflex action.

Your pickup, although important, is relatively simple. The same principles apply as in sprinting full speed, except that during your pickup to full speed you lengthen each stride and you adjust your body lean to your stride length. This means that if you were almost upright when you had to burst into a sprint you need to lean forward more than when you are in full stride. Therefore, the skill of your pickup lies in quickly assuming the correct body lean and beginning with short steps.

In a game like soccer or basketball or tennis you spend some time standing and waiting to make a quick burst of speed. You should be partially crouched so that your body angle will be closer to the extreme lean you need for the fastest start and pickup. Your first movement should be with the foot farthest away from the direction you want to go, but at the same time your body should turn in that direction and lean more. If you practice those principles your reflex action will give you a much faster start and pickup.

Endurance

There are many kinds of endurance, and the lack of any one kind can cause you to lose.

In considering exactly how this applies to you, a little knowledge of physiology might help. Think of your muscle cells as little engines. They can do their work as long as they have fuel and oxygen, but instead of gasoline they need carbohydrates. Your muscles store some fuel and a tiny amount of oxygen for instant reactions, but for much of their fuel and almost all the oxygen you must rely on your blood.

The first kind of endurance to consider is *aerobic*. Most of your endurance falls into this category. The word aerobic means "with oxygen," so aerobic work is what you can do using the oxygen supplied by your blood. When you move fast enough to begin puffing you are going beyond aerobic exercise into *anaerobic*, which means "without oxygen." Actually, you are using all the oxygen your blood can supply, but that is not enough so you must go into oxygen debt. Your anaerobic work is done chemically, and the amount you can go into debt is strictly limited. Even if you avoid anaerobic debt, a long session of aerobic exercise will deplete your *glycogen* supply, the fuel stored in your muscles. Loss of glycogen causes a marathon runner to "hit the wall" and a tennis player to lose some of his skill near the end of a long five-set match. Your muscles may also fail to get enough blood supply because you do not have enough *capillaries* carrying blood to them or because your *hemoglobin* is low and so does not carry enough oxygen. Another muscle failure results from lack of *strength*, because a weak muscle must work closer to its maximum capacity and so it goes into oxygen debt sooner.

If you lack aerobic endurance you will "run out of gas" in basketball, soccer, boxing, tennis, hockey, and, of course, distance running. You might even lose something in such a mild sport as golf if you play for four or five hours.

Your aerobic endurance is really a combination of physiological functions because it is greater with a full blood supply and a full fuel supply, but the basic tool is your heart. If you do anything that increases your pulse rate for several minutes most days, you heart will adapt to the added work by growing larger and stronger. It will then be able to pump more blood with each beat, which accounts for the lower pulse rate of trained endurance athletes. Therefore, your method of training for aerobic endurance is to be active often. The maximum gain would probably come from running for about half an hour a day at the fastest pace that would not push you far into oxygen debt. You would improve your aerobic endurance greatly with such a training schedule. For most sports that is enough, although a distance runner runs more in hopes of improving faster.

With aerobic training, your muscles keep demanding more blood and you grow more capillaries within the muscles you use regularly. A swimmer and a middle-distance runner develop similar aerobic capacities, but a swimmer tires rapidly when he tries to run because his running muscles have not developed enough capillaries to receive all the blood they need. Make certain you repeat all your movements enough to grow all the capillaries you need. A tennis player who never serves except when playing will find it tiring to serve long games. If a boxer did not spend hours holding his arms up while punching the bags, he would be too tired to fight more than a round or two.

Another way your muscles fail to obtain enough oxygen is when your hemoglobin level drops. Hemoglobin makes up about 95 percent of the dry weight of your red blood cells and carries most of the oxygen in your blood. Red blood cells are destroyed regularly in everyday living, and hard training destroys them much faster. If you do not replace these destroyed cells you will die. A hemoglobin value of 14 is all right for the average person, but an endurance athlete needs a value of 16 to 17 to perform well. You can build up your hemoglobin value in several ways: (1) Rest after hard training, which means at least two days of light work before a long competition. (2) Eat a balanced diet of fresh, unrefined foods that provide plenty of iron. (3) Live at high altitude. (4) Don't overtrain. You can check your blood values best with a blood test, but if you are aware of the problem you should consider the possibility whenever you feel run down.

Your anaerobic capacity allows you to go into oxygen debt, but that capacity is limited. A topnotch sprinter cannot run at full speed more than about 300 yards. You should not try to improve your anaerobic endurance until you have enough aerobic capacity to handle the training. Sports physiologists have determined that an otherwise well-trained runner can develop his anaerobic capacity to the maximum in five weeks. Since such hard training can lower your hemoglobin value and cause other problems, you should avoid all-out anaerobic training until just before you need it. You have some of the chemical capacity for going into oxygen debt simply by being alive and healthy. Even the most poorly trained person can sprint a short distance. You develop much more of it during your aerobic training. If you do speed training that takes you beyond your aerobic capacity you are also doing anaerobic training, and for most sports that is enough. Not everybody has the determination to train like Roger Craig, nor could many people stand it.

Roger Craig, offensive player of 1988 in the NFL, trains hard: In the spring of 1988 he rose at 6:30 to run 4 to 8 miles on a hilly course at a 7:00 mile pace uphill and under 6:00 downhill, three days a week — excellent aerobic training. Continuing to train like a track man, he ran on the track on three other days. He did 15 sprints of 100 yards, then ran 220 sprints with 30 seconds of rest between each — probably more than enough anaerobic training. During the season he sprints to the end zone each time he carries the ball in practice, and he runs sprint intervals after a game.

Glycogen is fuel, and each of your muscles stores a supply of it. When you run out of glycogen, usually after more than two hours of competition, you are dependent upon blood sugar, and most of your energy will come from burning fat. This is not as efficient as carbohydrates, so you cannot move as fast. Even worse, your central nervous system feeds on carbohydrates, so when you run short of glycogen your skills in any sport begin to fail.

To increase your glycogen supply, you should begin by increasing your capacity. That is done by exhausting your supply. If you train or compete until you run short of glycogen, as in running 20 miles, your capacity will increase. Then you need to fill your capacity by eating carbohydrates — which is why marathoners eat so much pasta before a race — and by resting. You should abstain from glycogen-burning activity for at least two days to allow your tank to fill.

The last aid to endurance has been discussed under *strength*. A weak muscle has to work harder to do the same job, thus requiring more fuel and oxygen.

Most sports are not considered to be endurance sports, but in most it is possible to become tired enough to lose your skill. Don't let it happen to you.

Skills

In many sports, training your skills is even more important than training for strength, speed, or endurance. If it came down to hitting a wedge shot close to the pin you'd pick a fat old golfer over the most highly trained marathoner or tennis champion.

Skill is what you need to shoot a basket, hit a backhand, complete a pass, bunt a baseball, or kick a goal. Each sport requires special skills, although some, like golf, depend almost entirely upon skills. In any case, you cannot succeed in sports without developing skills. To learn how to go about it, first learn something about your body.

One of the great wonders of your body is something we might call your Control System, a combination of at least four neuromuscular skills: *Kinethesia* is your sense of the position of your body. You know, without seeing, the location of each part. *Coordination* is your remarkable ability to use your nerves to control exact movements of your muscles, whether the tiny but complicated movements of writing your name or the large and also complex movement of swinging a bat to hit a fast-moving ball. *Memory* is what you need to perform coordinated movements exactly, time after time. *Reflexes* are like commands given by some unseen being; before you have time to think, your reflex puts into motion your correct action, as in balancing on a bicycle.

Your Control System is what performed the magic feat of learning to ride a bicycle. Somehow it discarded all your clumsy moves and retained only those that allowed you to regain your balance before your conscious mind even knew you were losing it. Nobody knows exactly how all this works, but they know you can learn almost any skill if you use your Control System properly.

The simplest way to train your Control System is to give it a goal. For an example, think about throwing a frisbee. If you did not have the goal of throwing it straight, you would not care how much it curved. But if you want to learn to throw it straight, then any other throw is rejected and not remembered by your Control System. In other words, give yourself a goal and your Control System will, by trial and error, gradually approach perfection.

There is one serious fault with this trial-and-error method: Your goal may not be the correct one. A tennis player teaching himself may be satisfied with the goal of returning every backhand. As a beginner it is more satisfying to return 95 percent of your backhands, even though they are slow and short, than it is to hit crisp returns but miss half of them. Your problem is that after a year or so of success against other beginners you find that your steady backhand is too weak and your opponents pound it past you. The worst part is that your Control System has learned it, and now you have to unlearn it before you can learn a more correct backhand.

The most important lesson you can learn about acquiring a skill is: LEARN IT RIGHT. It can be fun learning a skill all by yourself. Often an inferior form is easier and faster to learn, so your initial success comes quicker. But a second- or third-best method will limit you, and sometime in the future you will regret taking the easiest path.

Therefore, the goal you give your Control System should be a clear picture of the best way to perform a skill. Here are six ways to do it:

A *coach* can teach you the most, especially if you are young. A really good coach can set your goals and act almost like your Control System in correcting your errors while at the same time inspiring you to learn more.

If you *observe good form*, your Control System can use it as your goal. Watch good players in the stadium or on television. Use the VCR to collect action pictures of good form and study the technique, in slow motion if possible. To become an expert on technique you begin by observing, but you must study what you observe.

You should *read* as part of your study of technique. Books or magazines can tell you why one technique is best and make you aware of small movements that you might miss in your observations. Words, along with pictures, can give you a mental blueprint and thus give your Control System a clear goal.

Think about your form. If you never think about it, how do you expect to know when it goes wrong? Thought is the bridge between information in the form of words or pictures and the final command to your Control System.

You begin to think when you try to figure out *why* a certain technique is better than another. You may see all the good tennis players bend their front knee while making a stroke, but it feels more comfortable to you to stand up straight. If you think enough to realize that your knee should be bent to allow your weight to move forward as you stroke, then your Control System will accept your command to bend your knee.

Even more important than that bridge between your observation and your command, thinking can give you answers. If you have a problem and cannot find the answer in a book or from your coach or on film, sometimes you can think it out. An example might be your golf swing. Suppose you are slicing your drives. You can think of the cause: The ball is spinning clockwise because you are swinging from the outside in and pulling your driver across the ball. You think and experiment until you learn that tucking your right elbow closer to your body before your downswing will correct the arc. That small inch or two would not show in a picture, but you could find it by thinking.

You can find most answers with common-sense physics, but you don't have to study physics. You do have to study every movement involved in every skill you want to learn. Go through the movement in your mind in slow motion, and think of each part of your body that has anything at all to do with the skill, including those parts you want to keep out of the way and relaxed. The more you study the skill, the more you will understand the best way to do it.

Another method of sending correct commands to your Control System is by *feel*. Once in a while, during practice or play, you will make a movement that feels exactly right. When you do, you should point this out to your Control System. Tell it, "That's the way I want to do it every time." It usually surprises an athlete to get a perfect result with so little effort, but that is the way perfection feels. When it happens, try to use it again.

You can also send messages to your Control System by *imagining*. It is easier if you have experienced the perfect movement, but if not, you can certainly imagine the perfect result. Scientific experiments have proved that people can improve at shooting free throws or throwing darts with no other practice but their imagination.

The reason behind such black magic is the fact that your Control System does not know whether the picture it receives is real or imaginary. Your body can react with all the symptoms of fright when you see a figure hiding in the shadows ahead, whether the figure is a mugger or a tree stump. Your unconscious mechanism reacts the same way in either case.

Ben Hogan, one of the greatest golfers of all time, saw every shot in his imagination before he hit the ball, trying to "feel" the shot. He was telling his Control System what to do.

Now you have a toolbox full of methods for teaching your Control System, but they are not enough to make you skillful. The one activity that will make you great is correct practice.

trying to beat you, whereas in ordinary practice someone is working *with* you. For example, in tennis practice the ball is hit where you expect it to be, but in a match your opponent is trying to do exactly the opposite. Therefore, instead of practicing your forehand on a waist-high shot with your feet perfectly positioned, you get a low twister that you have to hit on the run. You have learned the basic stroke, but difficult shots require adjustments, so competitive practice means experimenting with the right kind of adjustment for an unusual situation. If you are only trying to win you can return the difficult shot as safely as possible, but to practice you should try to hit it well. In other words, use a less desirable technique that needs practice instead of the one most likely to win.

A striking example of the difference between competition in a game and drill is seen in basketball foul shooting. Among top basketball players, anyone who sinks more than 80 percent of free throws is considered a good foul shooter. And yet an obscure player named Ted St. Martin set a world record for free throws by sinking 927 in a row. There should not be that much difference simply because you are in the midst of a game. This is an area where anybody, expecially the highly paid pros, should be able to improve immensely.

Possibly the most important consideration about skills is to learn correctly. Players who learn haphazardly almost always develop flaws. You can see flaws in professional players who succeed in spite of them, but how much better could they be? If you take pains to learn correctly from the start, you will save yourself much pain later on. Perhaps you'll even save your career.

Most people and many athletes think that practice me
nothing more than trying to perform the skill you want to lea
In reality, practice can be divided into four kinds.

First you practice to learn your skill. You use one or all d
the methods for teaching your Control System what to do, and
you work at it until you can do it correctly. That includes
selecting the right way to do each part of it and putting the parts
together into the whole movement. In the tennis forehand, for
example, you learn the grip, the footwork, the backswing,
timing of your stroke, and the follow-through. When you can
do each of those correctly, put them together and work on the
whole stroke.

Next, after learning to make the whole stroke reasonably
well, you practice to perfect it. That means drill. You must do it
over and over again until you can do it almost perfectly and do
it the same way each time. Some skills may require thousands
of hours of drill. Too many athletes never perfect their skills
because they cannot stand the drudgery of constant drill.

If you know you need more drilling but you dislike the chore,
there are ways to make it more interesting. Practicing with
others is usually more fun, and you might think about finding
the most pleasant place to practice. Concentration makes anything more interesting, and one of the best ways to concentrate
is to make your practice competitive. Compete against yourself. Keep records of your progress and keep trying to break
your record. And use variety by stopping one drill when you
seem to have it right and start on another skill.

Third, after you are satisfied, you practice for the purpose of
retaining your skill. That does not take much time compared
with your drilling stage. A few minutes twice a week should
retain most skills, or perhaps competition is all the refresher
you need. It is up to you to decide, based on results.

Your fourth and last type of practice is during competition. It
would be foolish to practice during an important match, but in
practice matches, unimportant games, or competition where
you can win easily, you should practice.

Competitive practice is different because your opponent is

Chapter V

How to Compete

When you have chosen the sport best suited to your natural talents and then have improved your condition as much as possible and learned all the skills you can, are you as good an athlete as you'll ever be?

The answer is, "No!" If your racing car is the best car in the race, you won't win with a poor driver. In an athletic competition your well-prepared body is like the car and your brain is like the driver. You need finely tuned mental control to be the best possible athlete.

Mental control is complicated, and if you leave it to chance it can be more than difficult: It can turn against you. You can try to simplify it and gain some control by dividing it into Planning, Emotional Control, and Concentration.

Planning

While you are competing you do not have time for careful thinking. Therefore, you should do as much planning as possible before the game begins. Make your plans calmly and objectively for every possible situation, and have them ready to put into action when each situation arises.

Your Control System will automatically execute each plan if you have told it exactly what to do. Indecision can cause you to use the wrong tool or use it improperly. For example, when your tennis opponent hits a short shot from the base line, you run for it and barely reach it. You have a choice of at least six shots to try, but you can't consider them all in your desperate rush to reach the ball. If you have made a decision beforehand to use an angled drop shot in this situation you will do it without thinking. If you try to think, you will probably try something else or even compromise with a weak tap back to your opponent.

Give your Control System exact orders. It cannot make decisions.

Begin your planning by collecting information. First you need information about yourself. You need to know all your strengths and weaknesses so that your plan favors your strengths. You need to know your capabilities. What is your percentage for each kind of shot? What will happen to you if you run the first 10 miles of a marathon at a 2:10 pace? Can you block a linebacker with a knee-high dive? You need this complete information about yourself in order to form your basic plan.

Your basic plan is what you will do under average circumstances if your opponents perform in the usual way. Thus, a tennis player might choose a hard, deep shot down the line as his normal forehand, ready to change it only for some good reason.

Next you need information about the site of your competition. The site does not change in bowling, but every golf course is different. Include the weather in this, because your tactics may have to change in rain or cold.

Information about your opponent is vital to planning for a boxing match, tennis, racing, or the team sports. The top teams obtain scouting reports containing all possible information about their opponents, but as an individual you may have to find your own information. In order of importance, you can obtain information from films, playing against your opponent, watching your opponent, scouting reports, written accounts of competition, and watching opponents warm up.

Use all your information to form your plan. Start with your basic plan and change it to fit the site and your opponents.

As soon as your plan is ready, begin to make alternate plans. You need another plan in case the weather changes. You want an alternate plan for any change in tactics by your opponent. You must be ready to change plans if any of your skills fail. When you have a complete set of alternate plans, you should begin your visualization. That means you imagine yourself in each situation and "see" yourself carrying out your plan. In this way you tell your Control System what to do no matter what happens. Al Oerter won his fourth Olympic gold medal in the discus when rain surprised the throwers in the 1968 Olympics. The others threw poorly, but Oerter threw better than ever because he had a plan for rain. He said, "I know ahead of time what I will do under every condition."

Jack Nicklaus, golf's greatest winner, outlined his visualization technique: "I never hit a shot, even in practice, without having a very sharp infocus picture of it in my head. It's like a color movie. First, I 'see' the ball where I want it to finish. Then the scene quickly changes and I 'see' the ball going there. Then there's a sort of fade-out, and the next scene shows me making the kind of swing that will turn the previous images into reality."

At least one alternate plan should be ready to avoid failure because of fatigue. Your plan should allow for pacing yourself over long contests, for using tactics that will shorten the time, for replenishing your glycogen supply by consuming glucose, and for making the proper changes when fatigue causes your skills to decline.

Emotional Control

Why do you suppose a football coach gives his team a stirring talk before the game? Why do football teams have cheerleaders? Why does the coach put a newspaper clipping on the bulletin board quoting some derogatory remark by an opponent?

The purpose is to excite the team. Excited players have more adrenaline flowing and are motivated to play harder. They ignore pain and fatigue. Football history is full of "fired-up" teams that have upset favored teams. Some of these upsets rank as miracles like that of a frail woman who lifted a car to free a child trapped under the wreckage.

Texas coach Darrell Royal said, "Only angry people win football games." And sportswriter Paul Gallico said, "Cruelty and absolute lack of mercy are essential qualities in every successful prizefighter." Even the very feminine Chris Evert said, "I have to get mad to win."

Athletes often try to "psych" themselves. They try to bring themselves to a state of excitement where they seem stronger and faster and more aggressive.

One way to do this is by using your emotions as energy. Whenever you feel an emotion, you have energy to go with it. If you can learn to use that energy you have a source of extra power.

As an example, Russian athletes are given autoconditioning training to help them "choose their moods and thoughts at will," according to Grigori Raiport, president of the Russian Success Method. Raiport was trained in futuristic sports techniques at the Moscow National Research Institute of Physical Culture. When inspired, Raiport says, athletes could feel "a tingling in the jaw, coolness in the temples, lightness in the body." He says that the Russians would have managed speed skater Dan Jansen properly. Jansen's sister died on the day he was to compete in the 1988 Winter Olympics. U.S. officials left him alone in his grief, and Jansen fell during his race. Raiport says, "Russians would have handled the tragedy differently. Realizing that any strong emotion possesses energy, they would have tried to transform the negative energy of grief into a constructive force. Instead of leaving Dan alone, they would have been with him all day, saying: 'You're going to do this for your sister. Imagine that she is watching you, that she is waiting for you at the finish line.'"

In sports where "hustle" can win, such added energy is beneficial. But when you use skills requiring accuracy, you do best when you are relaxed. It is possible to be fired-up and still be relaxed in the muscles necessary for your movements, but it is highly unlikely. A basketball player may save an out-of-bounds by diving into the crowd under the influence of excitement, but that same excitement will cause him to shoot poorly compared with his relaxed shots.

Relaxation is the opposite of tension, and tension is the cause of skill failure. Any emotion that causes tension, especially fear, will harm your skills. The great football coach Tom Landry said, "I don't believe you can be emotional and concentrate the way you must to be effective."

Once your skill is learned, your Control System executes it as well as you have learned it. Your skill will fail only if you interfere with your Control System.

One way to interfere is by thinking of your action while you do it. A novice artist tries to draw a line by concentrating hard and guiding each small movement of the brush. A good artist draws that same line with one quick, light stroke. The one draws crabbed, inaccurate lines, whereas the other draws straight and accurate lines. A relaxed and easy movement is more accurate and skillful.

Thus, the tension that causes poor performance can come from the tension of trying too hard or from the tension caused by emotion. Therefore, you should psych yourself up to an excited pitch only when accuracy is not necessary. A football lineman needs as much hustle as possible and no accuracy. A golfer needs exactly the opposite. It all depends upon the specific requirements of your sport and especially the particular situation.

It would be great if you could push one button to fire yourself up for the maximum performance and push another button to bring on the perfect relaxation you need for maximum accuracy. You can't do it with buttons, but it is possible to approach such an ideal condition.

In a situation when you want to psych yourself into an excited state of all-out effort, you might think of your mind as the jockey and your body as the horse. You need a psychological whip to excite yourself.

Your whip can be anything, as long as it works. Most athletes talk to themselves, silently or aloud. Some athletes berate themselves with scornful criticism when they do something wrong. That is not a good idea because your Control System does not function properly under negative input.

A "whip" can be a carrot or a stick. The carrot is incentive—something you want. The stick is punishment you want to escape by doing the right thing. If you use the stick you are making a threat, and such negative input will cause tension and reduce your skills. You will succeed far more often with the carrot type of whip. Give yourself an incentive that makes you excited about winning.

You can imagine yourself winning. Imagine the cheers of the crowd and the approval of your friends. Imagine receiving all the rewards of winning. Imagine seeing your name in headlines or being interviewed for television. Use your mind to give you reasons to play with great emotion and hustle.

But what if your situation calls for a calm, relaxed approach? Obviously, you cannot relax if you feel fear, worry, or anxiety. Nor can your Control System make a skillful movement if you try to guide yourself through it, slowly and carefully concentrating on each muscle. Once your Control System has learned a skill, you can only give it the order and let it take over completely.

If you do not completely believe this, try typing or playing the piano while thinking about each finger position. Or try riding a bicycle while consciously correcting every tiny imbalance with a movement of the front wheel. Your Control System has a shortcut to your nerves and muscles. It can do the job far faster and more accurately than you can do with your conscious mind.

Use your conscious mind to *decide.* Do you want to shoot for the basket or pass off to a teammate? Hit the tennis ball down the line or crosscourt? Plunge straight toward the tackler or try to sidestep? But once you have made the decision, let your Control System handle it. Never send your Control System any kind of message in the midst of a movement.

Thus, any kind of interruption may cause your Control System to send the wrong message. It can be a conscious thought at the wrong time, or it can be an emotion that causes tension in one or more of the muscles you need to make a skillful movement. To relax you must shut out those emotions.

You cannot shut out emotions simply by using your willpower and saying, "I won't fear anything." That's like telling yourself you won't think of a white elephant. The harder you try, the more you will find a white elephant slipping into your thoughts. You cannot do it negatively. The only way you can eliminate one thought is by substituting a more interesting thought, one that involves your mind so much that you don't think of anything else. It is like eliminating a small pain by inflicting a greater pain. The best way to eliminate negative thoughts or feelings is to have a strong positive thought or feeling.

The Power of Positive Thinking by Norman Vincent Peale dealt with this subject and its effect on your whole life. It is not easy to think positively all the time, but you should start now, whatever your age, trying to learn how.

The rewards can be great. One of the best examples of positive thinking in sports happened on the 17th green at Pebble Beach during the last round of the U.S. Open in 1982. Tom Watson was tied with Jack Nicklaus, who had already finished. Watson's tee shot on the 17th left him in the tall grass above the slick and sloping green. Watching on television, Nicklaus felt certain that Watson would not be able to stop the ball on his second shot close enough to sink the putt for a par. Watson's caddy pleaded, "Get it close."

Almost any golfer, even most of the pros, would concentrate on getting it close, fearing the ball would run on past by several feet. But Watson is different. He thinks positively. He told his caddy, "I'm going to sink it."

He studied the frightening situation once more, took his stance, and swung his club delicately. The ball popped out of the grass, rolled down the green, and dropped into the cup.

Bill Rogers, playing with Watson, called it "a thousand to one shot." Nicklaus was shocked. And once again, many people called Watson "the luckiest golfer alive."

But Watson has done it too many times for it to be nothing more than luck. He had already holed out from off the putting surface on the tenth and fourteenth holes! His positive attitude eliminates the tension that would bring about the shots other golfers fear. When he thought, "I'm going to sink it," he gave himself two advantages over his opponents.

First, he gave himself a target. He visualized the ball rolling into the cup, whereas others only visualized it stopping close to the cup. They usually hit their much easier target, but Watson sometimes hits his.

Second, Watson does not allow negative thoughts to block his Control System. He has invested countless hours of practice in teaching his Control System what he wants, and he does not prevent his Control System from working efficiently by tensing his muscles because of fear or other negative thoughts.

You should start doing some thinking about positive thoughts. One of your most important goals should be to give yourself the right philosophy about losing. Keep in mind that there are far more losers than winners in sports. Even the best of the professionals loses some of the time. Babe Ruth struck out far more often than he hit a home run. Losing is a fact of life in sports. If you are emotionally upset to a great degree every time you lose, you should not be in sports.

If you enjoy competition, if you like to improve your skills and make progress, if you can be proud of yourself for doing your best even though you lose, then you are on the right track toward emotional control.

If you can stand over a ten-foot putt and think, "I have everything to gain by sinking this putt, and really nothing to lose," you set yourself up for a pleasant bonus if you sink it and you avoid the childish, "cry-baby" feeling so many athletes show. But if you think, "I'll lose if I miss this putt," you set yourself up for unhappiness, not only at that moment but throughout most of your sports career. What's worse, that negative thought will cause you to miss many putts. You should regard winning as something nice happening to you, not something that is your just due.

Psychologists name two attitudes that can ruin an athletic career. "Fear of failure" is obvious. If winning becomes so important to you that you cannot enjoy losing, then your fear of losing will cause you to lose. The other attitude is not so obvious. "Fear of winning" harms many athletes. They block themselves from winning because then they will be expected to win again and they don't believe they can. In either case they fail because fear tightens their muscles at the wrong time.

Byron Nelson, one of the all-time great golfers, said, "Putting affects the nerves more than anything. I would actually get nauseated over three-footers, and there were tournaments when I couldn't keep a meal down for four days."

Your best emotional control is no emotion at all. If you give your Control System a command calmly and remain calm while it is carried out, you will perform as well as you do in practice. In fact, your Control System can help you stay calm!

You can learn to make physical relaxation automatic. That is hard to believe, but think about biofeedback. Scientists have proved, and many people have demonstrated to themselves, that people can control even their involuntary muscles. One of the easiest tests proving this involves the temperature of your fingers. A thermometer is attached to a finger to show the temperature. By thinking the right thoughts, you can raise or lower the temperature of your fingers. You can also relax the tension in your "frown" muscles, reduce or eliminate the pain from a migraine headache, lower your blood pressure, and any number of other feats that sound like miracles.

One of your most important long-range goals, good for far more than sports, should be to learn relaxation.

You can learn relaxation in four steps:

1. Learn the feeling of tension.
2. Learn to relax that tension consciously.
3. Learn to relax muscles while other muscles are in action.

4. Teach your Control System to begin that relaxation automatically, even when you are not conscious of it.

You can begin learning the feeling of tension by clenching your fist as hard as possible. That feeling is tension. Put your thumb and forefingers on opposite sides of your forearm. Feel how it tightens when you clench your fist.

Now practice relaxing tense muscles. Put your thumb on your biceps and your fingers on the back of your arm, feeling your triceps. When you clench your fist, you probably tighten both your biceps and your triceps. Now put the back of your hand on a table or on your knee and push down as hard as you can. The muscles on the back of your arm, your triceps, must tighten to force your forearm down, but your biceps probably tightened as well. Practice relaxing your biceps while tightening your triceps. Then put your hand under the table or under your leg and lift. Your triceps should be relaxed while your biceps are tight. Now clench your fist while both of those muscles are relaxed. When you can relax antagonistic muscles or unneeded muscles, you have learned the difference between tension and relaxation.

The third step is harder, mainly because it is more difficult to detect tension when there is movement. Start with clenching and unclenching your fist. Even though you have learned how to clench without tightening your biceps and triceps, you probably feel a little tightening in at least one of your triceps when you clench and unclench rapidly. Notice that you can control this rather easily when you think about it. Now try the same principle with one of your skill motions.

For example, a tennis player might swing a forehand stroke. Try to feel all the unnecessary muscles that tighten when you stroke. These unnecessary muscles may be in your legs, in your other arm, in your neck and torso, or in the arm you use. Are you tightening your biceps or triceps when you don't need them? This self-examination can take a lot of time and effort, but every unnecessary muscle you relax will improve your skill.

Sometimes, while you are practicing your skills, concentrate on relaxing unnecessary muscles. You won't conquer these bad habits in one day, but you will soon learn to relax unnecessary muscles while you are in action.

Now comes the fourth and last step. Up to this point it has been as if you pushed a button to correct something you notice. Now you want your Control System to push that button automatically. Your goal is to train your Control System to notice any unwanted tension and relax it.

Any muscle control you can do consciously is possible to do automatically. You teach your Control System through feelings in your muscles and through conscious thoughts or commands. You combine them by noticing proper relaxation and calling it to the attention of your Control System. You call attention to it by noticing each time it fails. When you learned to ride a bicycle, your goal was to ride straight. Each fall was wrong, so your Control System discarded it. Show your Control System your goal by relaxing all unneeded muscles consciously. Slowly but surely, your Control System will zero in on that goal until finally you won't have to think about it at all.

Even after your Control System has learned automatic relaxation, it is possible for you to override it by feeling a strong emotion that produces tension. It is not as easy to practice relaxation under emotionally caused tension because you first have to produce that emotion. The best way to do it is to wait until you feel the emotion or tension, then consciously relax and tell your Control System that that is what you want it to do. Some athletes try to simulate emotional situations while practicing by saying something like, "I have this putt for the Masters Championship." Lee Trevino did it unconsciously when he was young by betting on putting contests. "You don't know what pressure is until you play for five bucks with only two in your pocket."

You might try by practicing when you feel a strong emotion caused by something entirely different. There is no certain way to practice while tense, so you must try anything you think of, especially during competition.

If you can teach your Control System to eliminate tension

from your skill movements even when your natural inclination should leave you tense with fear, you will give yourself what may be the single most powerful competitive tool any athlete can have.

Concentration

Concentration means giving your attention to only one thing. If your concentration is on the *right* thing, it is of great value to you in sports and most other activities.

A six-year-old boy was trying to shoot baskets but missing more than he made. His coach told him about concentration. The boy squinted his eyes and took his time, and he made ten in a row.

Bill Bradley, one of the great pro shooters, always concentrated on the near edge of the rim. No matter where his body was moving, his eyes were anchored to the rim. It is the simplest and most exact way to point out your goal to your Control System.

You concentrate on different things in different sports and at different times in the same sport. In tennis, you watch the ball as it comes toward you and concentrate on meeting it at exactly the right spot. Immediately, your concentration changes to powering and guiding the ball with a strong follow-through. Then you concentrate on your opponent to learn as quickly as possible what kind of shot he will make. Once the ball leaves his racket, you concentrate again on the ball. Any lapse in your concentration can cause an error or a less than good shot. And after the point ends, you concentrate on something else, perhaps tactics or an analysis of your last point.

Think about the action in your sport. Decide where your concentration should be in each part:

Do you have a target? If so, your concentration should be on that target—the ball, if it is moving, or the exact point you want it to go in basketball, bowling, pitching, passing, hockey, or soccer. If your target is an opponent—as in football or boxing—concentrate on the part of him you want to reach. During the movement, that is your only concentration.

As soon as you finish that movement, concentrate on preparation for the next one. In a sport like boxing, this is immediate. In sports like golf and bowling, you have time to think. Intense concentration on your opponent allows you to anticipate his next move. Therefore, in tennis you concentrate on your opponent's body position and backswing in order to gain a step or two.

Between plays, switch your concentration to sending positive pictures and commands to your Control System so as to have full control over your emotions. If you let your mind wander between plays, you have little control. This should be the last thing you do before play continues. If you have extra time, you can begin by concentrating on tactics. Are you following your plan? If so, and if it is not working, should you change tactics?

Don't make the mistake many athletes make of berating themselves for their mistakes in judgment or errors of execution. Be as positive as you possibly can. Tell yourself something to do, not something not to do. You would be wise to memorize a checklist so that it comes into your mind whenever you need it, especially when you are tired or caught up emotionally in the competition. Your brain does not function fully under the stress of combat, and you can help it in this way. Keep your list simple:

Am I watching the ball (target)?
Am I hustling?
Am I sending only positive pictures to my Control System?
Am I using the right tactics?
Is each of my skills functioning well?
Am I pacing myself in order to keep playing at my best?

If you work on mental control by making plans, by learning a positive attitude, and by concentrating on the right thought at the right time, you will make the most of your natural talents and your training. If you are serious about your sport, you would be foolish to do any less.

Managing Your Amateur Sports Career

You know something about training and competing, but there is more. Most amateur athletes drift along, doing their best as competitors but leaving many important details to their parents, their coaches, or to chance. You can use the following list to remind yourself not to neglect these important duties.

Study

You need to study even if you think sports are the only thing worth your hard work. Do you want to be eligible to compete for your school teams? At the very minimum you must study enough to win passing grades. Do you want to work at some nonplaying job in pro sports? Obviously, you must learn enough to qualify. Have you considered what you will do after your sports career? Unless you amass a small fortune as an athlete and have no other ambition in life, you will want to work at something when your pro sports career ends at the age of twenty-five to forty. Why not do most of your studying *before* you retire?

Use All the Help You Can Get

Only a superhuman could think of succeeding in sports with no help from anybody. You need help from your parents, coaches, friends, and many others.

If your parents are not behind you, your sports career will be difficult if not impossible. Many parents forbid their children to play sports in which injuries are common. Some parents consider sports a waste of time. Some parents have preconceived notions about which sport their children should play. Some parents make plans for their children that do not include practice.

You need to sell yourself as an athlete. If your behavior is good, your parents will have no reason to punish you by depriving you of time for sports. If your classwork is good, they can't say you have to study instead. You should talk with them, letting them know how important sports are to you. Do what you can to get them behind you to the point where they encourage you rather than hinder you. In the worst possible situation, ask your coach to help influence your parents.

Your coach is of great importance. Many young athletes look up to their coaches as father figures, receiving and accepting more and better advice than from negligent parents. But before you put yourself in his hands entirely, you should evaluate your coach.

A coach is a teacher. He teaches you how to play your sport. As a beginner you won't be able to judge him fully as a teacher, but you should be aware that some high school coaches are academic teachers not fully prepared to be coaches. If he is unable to help you learn, you should try to learn from somebody else without jeopardizing your place on the team. Sometimes you can find a former athlete or even another coach to help you. Or you might help yourself by reading or watching films.

A coach may be bad because he is over critical instead of encouraging, or because he advocates winning by cheating, or because he plays favorites, or risks injuries. Supportive parents may be able to help you in such cases. In an extreme case, you might be wise to take up another sport.

Whether your coach is great or poor, you should study your sport. You should do all you can to become an expert in each of the skills you need to know—in tactics, in psychology, in mental control, in everything that might give you the slightest edge.

The most important step in learning anything is to *want* to learn. If you really want to learn, you will read. You will listen to your coach and other players. You will watch games, live or on television, and study every move. You will ask questions and look for extra coaching. Most of all, you will think. Ask yourself *WHY*. Why is it better to bend your front knee in a tennis stroke? Why do you try to see the ball strike your bat in baseball? Why is the position of your right elbow important in your golf swing?

The more you want to learn, the more you will study and the more you will learn. And the more you learn, the better you will be.

To help yourself want to learn, you might start by setting goals. A goal can be many things. A goal can be something you want, such as to be voted into the Hall of Fame. A goal can be a contract with yourself, such as, "I will run five miles every day." Goals can be steps in your progression, such as, "I want to be able to press 200 pounds by February and 250 pounds a year later." A goal can be as short-range as, "I will try to swim a mile tomorrow," or as long-range as, "I will go into coaching for the rest of my life." A goal can be anything you want it to be.

Goals should be serious. Don't set a goal you do not intend to reach, because then you will form the habit of ignoring goals whenever it is easier to do so. Be careful about changing goals; don't change just because the new one is easier to reach.

Goals should include long-range goals and short-range goals, arranged so that the short-range are stepping-stones toward your ultimate goals. Enjoy your success each time you reach another goal.

Goals should be recorded. If you write it down, it is easier to remember and it will constantly remind you to go after it. If you tell somebody else your goal, you will have extra incentive to strive for it.

Use a set of goals to guide you and to motivate you.

Control Your Life-Style

Surely, you know enough to say no to drugs. Nobody with any common sense would grab a few hours of pleasure while risking bodily harm, death, loss of playing ability, expulsion from your sport, and a prison sentence. But do you know the dangers of steroids?

Somebody will tell you that steroids will make you a champion. They'll tell you that steroids will make you bigger and stronger. They'll say you can't compete with the best unless you take steroids.

Before you take their advice or their steroids, you'd be smarter to get the facts:

1. Don't mess with Mother Nature. Anabolic steroids are synthetic hormones. Natural hormones are produced in some of your cells, and they go to other cells to excite a specific effect. Examples are the fight-or-flight reaction to adrenaline and the sexual arousal by the sex hormones. Synthetic hormones produce unnatural reactions in your body, and they interfere with your natural reactions. People who like themselves should be wary of anything foreign to their natural bodies, whether it is drugs, cigarettes, asbestos, fats, polluted water, infected people, drunken drivers, or steroids. If you are a male, steroids can produce acne, make you bald, give you breasts like a girl's, and shrivel your testicles so you have no sex drive and cannot become a father. If you are female, you risk masculinization—loss of hair on your head while growing a beard, shrunken breasts, gross genital growth, and a deep voice. A study published in the *Journal* of the American Medical Association estimates that half a million high school seniors take steroids, with a third of them beginning by the age of fifteen. Particularly bad for young athletes is the fact that steroids can halt your growth before you reach your full height.

One of Russia's female Olympic athletes said, "My whole hormonal system is destroyed, my health is runied...and my life is still ahead of me. I would have liked to become a mother."

2. Steroids can be hazardous to your health. You risk cancer

of the liver, hepatitis, and leukemia. You might suffer kidney failure or heart attacks. Glen Maur, former champion body-builder, had a heart attack at the age of thirty-three. David Jenkins, an Olympic silver medalist in 1972 and now convicted of directing an international steroid smuggling operation, says, "There is the potential for fatal results and that's the scary thing, so what you're dealing with is a loaded gun."

3. Steroids can ruin your personality. They call it 'roid rage because it is caused by steroids and makes you anxious and hostile and violently aggressive, and sometimes it makes you a criminal. In an article in *Sports Illustrated*, Tommy Chaikin, a four-year football letterman at South Carolina, tells how steroids made him violent and caused such anxiety attacks that he decided upon suicide. "I was sitting in my room...with the barrel of a loaded .357 Magnum pressed under my chin....It had all come down from the steroids, the crap I'd taken to get big and strong and aggressive so I could play this game that I love."

4. It's against the law. Steroids are illegal without a prescription. Olympic sports require testing of participants, and users are banned. Ben Johnson, who won the 1988 Olympic 100 meters in world-record time, tested positive for a banned substance. He lost his gold medal and his world record; he was banned for two years, thus losing more than a million dollars worth of contracts; and he went home in disgrace. Other sports are following suit, including the National Football League.

5. It's against your conscience. If you like yourself, you don't want to think of yourself as a cheater. You'll take more pride in yourself if you can play well without artificial aid.

6. It's costly, in more ways than one. If you buy steroids on the black market, you can't be sure you are buying what you want. David Jenkins says, "We came to the conclusion that out of about every twenty purchases of steroids carried out in a gym or on the black market, probably nineteen of those would be counterfeit in some form." You can buy high-quality American steroids, but you need a prescription and money. A single injection can cost as much as $300, and pills can cost as much as $175 a month.

7. The odds are against you. Many people have gained weight and strength from steroids, but only some of them have achieved great athletic success. Many athletes have been successful without using steroids. If you weigh the uncertainty of fabulous success now against the certainty of unfavorable side effects in the future, a wise decision would be a vote for your future.

This choice—immediate gratification vs. future success—will require decisions from you for the rest of your life, but at no time are those decisions as difficult as in your teens. That is because you have not fully developed your self-discipline and the attractions are so intense. The sooner you begin to make choices favoring your future, the sooner you'll have a future favoring you. This kind of advice is all around you, but only you can decide what to do about it. Unless you think about each temptation and make a decision about how much of your future you want to sacrifice for each minute of pleasure, you will drift along with the crowd and probably complain later that the odds were against you.

Your life-style may well be the biggest choice you'll ever make.

Specialization

If you start high school with several sports on your schedule, the time will come when you must make a decision to specialize. Let's say you are an all-round athlete in junior high. You are the running back on the football team, forward on the basketball team, and in the spring you are center fielder on the baseball team and a sprinter on the track team. You are good in golf and tennis and play some soccer when you have time. You also like to play racquetball and bowl, and you'd like to try other sports. Obviously, you have to cut down on some of those.

It would be easy for you to go out for football, basketball, and baseball in high school. You could play golf and tennis on weekends and in the summer. If you were fast enough, you might sneak into a few sprint races along with playing baseball. Glenn Davis managed both while he was at West Point. If you had any energy left, you could fit in an occasional evening of bowling or racquetball. To play soccer you would have to give up another sport. But even if you were good enough to play all those sports, there are drawbacks.

First, such a schedule would leave little time for other activities. You would have to reduce the time you spent in studying, socializing, reading, and even watching television. Your life would be too one-sided. Second, you would have no time for out-of-season training in your sports. A basketball player must practice the year round to be a star. Third, you would probably go stale from constant training and competition. Rest is an important ingredient in preparing to compete, and you would have no rest.

On the other hand, if you cut out some sports you may eliminate your best chance for the future. For example, you may be a basketball star now and so you eliminate soccer. But if you only grow to be 5'll" tall, your chances are slim in college and pro basketball. Or you may have been playing baseball since you were eight but only began tennis last year. How can you judge your relative ability with one year's experience against six or seven years?

That is a real problem, but it may not be as difficult as it seems. For one thing you are probably not good in all sports. If you start out with high school football and learn that you are a little light and you are not sure you like the heavy pounding and it looks as if you will barely make the team, why not stop and begin practicing for basketball or tennis? Somewhere between your first day in high school and the start of your senior year, you should decide to specialize.

Most athletes are scholarship material in no more than one sport. You should be able to identify that sport during your junior year. Then you can devote all your training time to one sport and develop much faster than if you play it only during the season. Here again, it is a choice between present pleasure and your future. If you love basketball but your future is in baseball, you can play in intramural or pick-up basketball games for fun but concentrate year round on developing your baseball skills.

It will be easy enough for you to concentrate on your main sport and still keep your hand in at golf or tennis for fun and for future recreation. Your goal is to improve as much as possible in your main sport. And you should do so for at least a year before you expect to win a scholarship. Great success in sports, as in most things, comes to those who give it close to 100 percent in effort. You cannot keep up with those athletes if you devote only 25 percent of your year's effort to one sport. Sooner or later you must specialize, and it should be no later than your senior year of high school.

Pursue a Scholarship

For almost every good high school athlete, one of the most important goals is to win a college scholarship. If you are offered an athletic scholarship, it means that somebody thinks enough of your prospects to give you board, room, books, and fees worth about $5,000 a year plus tuition worth anywhere from $1,500 at a state university to $15,000 at a private college or university.

The money and prestige involved make it worth your efforts, which means you should do more than merely play well.

Before you begin to think seriously about a scholarship, you should know something about the general situation. More than 3,000 colleges in the United States are divided into four-year institutions, whose athletic competition is governed by either the NCAA or the NAIA, and two-year institutions governed by the NJCAA. The National Collegiate Athletic Association in turn is divided into divisions, with Division I including the powerhouses of college sports. Therefore, Division I is the first choice of most of the best athletes, although many professionals come from Division II or from the smaller colleges of the NAIA.

Each of those organizations allows its colleges a certain number of scholarships for each sport. For example, until the

MANAGING YOUR AMATEUR SPORTS CAREER   **65**

next changes, Division I colleges are allowed to give the
following number of scholarships:

	Men	*Women*
Baseball	13	
Basketball	15	15
Fencing	5	5
Field hockey		11
Football	95	
Golf	5	6
Gymnastics	7	10
Ice hockey	20	
Lacrosse	14	11
Rifle	4	
Skiing	7	
Soccer	11	
Softball		11
Swimming	11	14
Tennis	5	8
Track & X-C	14	16
Volleyball	5	12
Water polo	5	
Wrestling	11	

You need to know the rules involved in a scholarship,
including rules concerning eligibility, recruiting, and financial
aid.

You can hinder or ruin your college career in several ways.
Your first eligibility hurdle is academic. Under the new Division I rules, to be eligible as a freshman you must graduate with
a C average in at least eleven full academic courses, including
three years of English and two each of mathematics, social
science, and natural or physical science. You must score at least
700 on the SAT or 15 on ACT. For Divisions II and III you
must meet that college's requirements and be a full student. To
transfer from a two-year college you must graduate or have
acceptable grades. A new and controversial rule, adopted by

the NCAA in 1989, denies scholarships to any high school athlete who fails to meet the standards of a C average and 700 score.

Another eligibility hurdle is amateurism. In the NCAA you are allowed to be a professional in one sport and retain your amateur standing in another. You must be an amateur in your scholarship sport, which means that you cannot sign a contract, secret or otherwise, in that sport. You are also ineligible if you sign a contract with an agent who will represent you later. Some agents have been known to risk their athlete's whole career by offering a secret contract, whispering, "Nobody will ever know." You will also be declared ineligible if you appear in commercials or give endorsements for products. You cannot allow your name to go into the pro draft.

The rules for recruiting are rigid and severe. Many athletes have suffered because they allowed an ignorant or cheating recruiter to break the rules. You cannot be expected to be up-to-date on all the rules, especially since they change from time to time, but you can learn some. And whenever a recruiter offers you something or takes you for a visit, ask if it is against any rule.

The most common recruiting rules have to do with "contacts." If a recruiter visits your home, that is a contact. If the visit is at your school, that is a contact. A recruiter may not contact you more than three times at home and three times at school. Alumni are not allowed to contact you anywhere except on the college campus. You are allowed five visits to colleges, with all expenses paid, but each visit must last less than forty-eight hours.

Later, when you decide which scholarship to accept, you will sign a letter of intent. This letter is like a contract between you and the college, signaling the end of recruiting. After you have signed, no other college can recruit you. If you change your mind and go to another college, you will lose eligibility. On the other hand, once you have signed there is no longer any limit to the number of contacts you may receive.

The third set of rules applies to your scholarship. The financial aid you receive is limited to tuition, room and board, fees, and books. You are permitted no employment except during vacations. You will receive complimentary tickets to games, but these are for your friends and relatives. If you sell them, you risk losing your eligibility.

Everybody has read news stories about superathletes being given gifts, some as expensive as a house or car. Probably many thousands of athletes have sold comps. Alumni have been known to give money to athletes. Favors are extended ranging from introducing girls to finding a job for the athlete's father. All are against the rules, and the police force of the NCAA is always on the job, waiting to pounce.

The penalties to a college or university are harsh. Oklahoma University was placed on probation for three years, beginning in 1989. The school is not allowed to play in bowl games for two years nor receive television money in 1989. It can recruit only eighteen football players per year instead of twenty-five. The school estimates that it will lose close to a million dollars a year. All this because some alumni cheated by giving money to players, who also cheated by taking it. You can harm your college by breaking the rules.

Your own penalties can be severe. You can be declared ineligible ever to play for that college. You may lose your scholarship and your degree. The college may be placed on probation, ineligible to play in postseason playoff games.

In spite of these punishments, rules are broken for many reasons, mainly money and pride. Millions of dollars are involved in college football. A winning team can mean hundreds of thousands of dollars to its college. Winning or losing means that the coach keeps his job or is fired. Wherever big money is involved some people cheat, and sports, unfortunately, are no exception. In addition to money, pride in the team causes some people, expecially alumni, to break the rules.

To protect your good name, your honor, and your future, you must know the rules and obey them.

In addition to the rules, you should have some idea of how the recruiting process is carried out and how it will affect you.

First, some college must become interested in you as a prospective student and athlete. If you are all-state or state champion, you have no problem. They all know of you, and many of them will try to recruit you if your other qualities are high enough. But what if you are in the much larger category of high school athlete—good but not great? Most of the colleges in your area will know about you, but you may be after larger game. How do you gain their attention?

Your first step in selling yourself is to be realistic about how high you aim. Do you and your coach honestly believe that you can make any college team in the country? Or are your hopes no better than Division III? Don't waste your time trying for a football scholarship at Notre Dame or USC if you did not make your league all-star team.

Look for several colleges on a level where you should be able to play. Whether you have fifty recruiters beating a path to your door or none at all, you should consider a lot more than a college's won-lost record. After all, your college is where you spend at least four years of your life, where you make lifetime friends and shape your future forever. Don't make the choice lightly.

Of course you want the best athletic program you can find. Usually the big Division I schools have the top programs, the best coaches and facilities, and the best competition, but that is not always true. Some smaller colleges have coaches you'd rather have. Some fancy facilities are great on quantity but not better in the quality you want.

You will be better off in a college where athletes are given some sort of study supervision. You need a "brain coach" as well as a baseball coach. What percentage of freshmen graduate? What percentage of athletes in your sport? Does this college continue to help athletes after their eligibility runs out? Unless you are a poor student and do not expect to improve, you should consider the academic reputation of the college as well as its athletic reputation. Does it have the courses you want for your major?

Consider other aspects of college life. Do you like the players and students? Are your favorite recreations available? What are your chances for a summer job? Does the college offer help in finding a job? How far from home is the college, and do your parents like it or dislike it?

After you have looked into several colleges, you will prefer certain ones. These are the colleges where you want to be considered for a scholarship. Your next step is to attract their attention and interest.

The best and easiest method is probably through your coaches. Sometime in your junior year of high school you should let them know you would like to earn a scholarship. A coach who likes you and thinks you are good enough can be of great help. Coaches have contacts at some colleges and can tip them off to watch you. Coaches can give you advice and even add one or more colleges to your list.

Some high school athletes contact colleges of their choice by mail or in person to let them know of their interest. Photo copies of nice write-ups in your local newspaper might help. One of the best-selling aids is to show film of your best play. Many high schools film their games, and you could copy some of your best moves. If the school does no filming, you might borrow a camcorder and let your parents film your games.

You, or somebody else, must put on a public relations campaign in your behalf. Once you are known to a college coach, he can decide if he is interested. If he is, a recruiter will check your qualifications. If nothing turns him off, a recruiter will travel to interview you.

Before talking with you, the recruiter will stop in the school office to check on your grades and any information about your general reputation. If all is well, the recruiter will visit your coach and collect information about your natural ability, your training efforts, and your strengths and weaknesses as a player and as a person.

Then, when the recruiter talks with you, it is time for you to sell yourself. This will be like a job interview, and you want to behave well so as to make a good impression. Don't turn the recruiter off with bad manners, bragging, shyness, coarseness, or any other suspect behavior. If you are in doubt, ask your coach for advice on how to act.

Take notes on each recruiter and whatever promises he makes. Have all your records available so that you can answer all questions. Your athletic notebook or training diary can help you remember such things as how much weight you gained in the last year or your marks in the 40-yard dash or the standing spring for height.

During this interview you may collect information about the college or its athletic program. You can ask such questions as, "Do you have a weight training coach? What is policy about conflicts between training or games and classes or lab schedules?" You can also make a judgment about the honesty and character of the recruiter.

If your chances are still good, the recruiter may want to visit your home. A good family relationship as sures the recruiter of your stability. If you have been properly impressive, the recruiter may at this time make you an offer. If so, take careful notes on exactly what is offered. Don't accept the statement, "full ride," without asking exactly what it covers. The official scholarship statement does not come until *after* you make your decision and sign the letter of intent. Therefore, you want an exact verbal statement before you make your decision.

Instead, you may be offered a campus visit first. This expenses-paid trip will give you a chance to see the entire campus including the athletic facilities. You will probably meet the head coach and consider his style. You can talk with other players and students. They may take you to a game or a party. The more they do for you, the more interested they are and the more critical should be your judgment so as to be able to compare them with the next college.

You should prepare yourself to be able to handle any recruiting pressure. If, instead of having to sell yourself to them, they are trying to sell themselves to you, then you know you have a choice. Ask how long you have to make up your mind. If there *are* competing colleges, letting them know will strengthen your position.

If, on the other hand, this is the only college interested in you, don't delay. If you want to attend that college, be enthusiastic and let them know you are favorably impressed. Most colleges recruit more athletes than they can sign. If you hold them off, they may come up with your replacement before you decide.

If you are not offered a scholarship immediately, keep trying. Bill Serra of College Athletic Placement Service in Asbury Park, N.J., says, "The athletic-scholarship world is like an iceberg. Only the tip is showing." He claims a 90 percent success rate in finding "rides" for about 500 men and women each year, but he charges a retainer fee of $400 plus $1,000 for placement. Serra says, "Every year, grants go begging for lack of candidates."

If you fail to win a scholarship, it does not mean the end of your athletic career. There are other forms of financial aid. At some colleges and universities more than 75 percent of the students qualify for financial aid and almost all are accepted on the basis of need. Once you are in college, almost all teams will accept walk-ons. That means you can try out for the team without being on scholarship. You have your chance to prove yourself.

Succeed in College

Too many athletes go to college only to pursue their ambition of becoming professionals. They waste a great opportunity because college gives students a much larger future income, the ability to learn whatever they need in their lives, and knowledge that will enrich their lives and make them far more useful.

To be given a scholarship for a college education is like being given $40,000 to $80,000 and directed how to use it wisely. To waste it is foolish. Only a little over one third of NFL players have graduated. This means that after their short NFL career they either have to return to college or make a living without a college degree. Make graduation one of your main goals.

If your sport requires so much time that you cannot keep up with a full classload, make it up in summer school. Take a full load of the more difficult courses during your off season.

Another main goal is success in your sport. In addition to your training and competition, there are important considerations that can help or hurt you.

Learn the system and the people. That means learning all the rules and obeying them. Avoid ticket-scalping, even though your teammates pick up such illegal money. Stay away from agents, even when they promise you nobody will ever know if you sign an illegal contract. Do not accept illegal gifts that might cause you to lose your eligibility. Consider changing your position. If you are only third string at quarterback and you believe you can play first string as a wide receiver, don't let pride stand in your way.

Reduce your chance of injury. Don't risk injury by playing when you are in poor condition. Stay in condition all year. You are also more liable to injuries if you loaf or play carelessly. And when you *are* injured, be wary of painkillers.

One horror story about painkillers is told by the great basketball center Bill Walton: "At halftime, Dr. Cook said if I just took this shot of Xylocaine in my leg, it would be all right to go back out and play. I took the shot, felt good for about thirty-five seconds, limped through the rest of the game, and spent the next six weeks in a cast on crutches."

Avoid being run off. Sometimes a coach may decide he doesn't like you. Maybe he thinks you are not good enough, even though you are still only a freshman. He may want to turn your scholarship over to another player. He may try to make you quit by various methods including ridicule and letting you sit on the bench. If you believe in yourself, don't let him run you off. Try all the harder, and make the other players like you and take your side.

Getting along in college means concentrating on being a good student and a good person. Work at it the way you work at your sport.

Monitor Your Progress

When you make any play in your sport you think you will remember it. You think you will remember how it felt and why it went wrong, or right. But you won't remember everything. For example, in a round of golf you will swing many different clubs many times. If you keep a record of each stroke you lose and why you went wrong, you can check it over later to learn which shots you need to practice the most. A year later you will be able to compare yourself now and then and know how much progress you are making.

If you practice shooting free throws every day, your memory will not tell you your percentage improvement a year later. If you are a runner, a log of your workouts will help you decide why you were particularly good or bad in various races.

Therefore, you should keep an athletic diary. You should have an entry for each day. Even if you do nothing, you should make a note of why you were idle. You should enter the time of your workout, weather conditions, personal conditions such as your weight, pulse rate, hours of sleep, and any illness or injuries. You should record your workouts or game performances and make subjective thoughts about your progress. You can add notes about anything that might help you. Enter anything to aid your memory.

One way to monitor your progress is to write down each of your goals, whether short-term or long-term. Then write down how close you came to reaching your goals. This not only acts as a checklist to remind you of your target, but it keeps a record of your successes.

You should keep a list of roadblocks to progress. What caused you to fall short? Was it lack of skills or knowledge, bad decisions, poor conditioning, injuries?

Use your notebook diary as a sort of third eye with which you can stand off and look at yourself objectively as if you were your own coach.

Decision

Toward the end of your college career you need to make a decision. Will you attempt to become a pro? It may be an easy decision because it is obvious that you are not good enough. If such is the case you will already know it, and the decision will be made. The only danger is that you may believe you are better than you are. On the other hand, if you are obviously good enough your decision will be easy unless you are balancing another career against pro sports. Somewhere in the middle you may decide you have some chance of gaining a professional contract. Then it is up to you. If you decide to try, it means hard work and the chance of failure. It may mean temporarily suspending your pursuit of another career and even putting off marriage. Still, you have much to gain and your small losses should be only temporary.

Chapter VII

Breaking in as a Professional

If you are a superior athlete you will have no trouble breaking in as a pro. In individual sports you will be good enough to qualify for the top tournaments, and in team sports you will be drafted. All you need is a good agent and knowledge of the rules.

But if you are borderline, like most excellent college athletes, you need more. You also need to know how and where you can prove yourself good enough to be a pro.

In every sport you must work your way up until you are one of the best amateurs. Even then, in most sports, you must showcase your abilities to attract a pro contract. Your best opportunity to show off your abilities is in your school competition, but sometimes that is not enough. If you attend a small high school or an obscure college your achievements may go unnoticed. Since most sports differ from each other, you should examine your chosen sport carefully to learn how to show off your ability to the best advantage.

All the team sports conduct a draft. The pro teams get together at least once a year and make their choices among all the available unsigned players, mostly from the colleges. The draft is your mainstream avenue of approach to a professional contract, but it is not the only way. Most sports offer other opportunities. By the time you are ready to break in as a pro, you should know how to go about it in your particular sport.

Team Sports

BASEBALL: The highest salaries for athletes are paid in baseball. The minimum salary increases each year with the cost of living. In 1989 it rose to $68,000. Of the SPORT 100 for 1986 — a list of the 100 highest-paid athletes — 68 were baseball players. In 1987 ten players were paid at least $2 million. The *average* salary in 1988 was $438,729, according to the Major League Baseball Players Association. The highest-paid player in 1988 was Ozzie Smith of the St. Louis Cardinals, who received $2.34 million.

In 1989 salaries escalated again. Dwight Gooden of the New York Mets signed a contract calling for a 1989 salary of $2,416,667. Cal Ripken of the Baltimore Orioles topped Gooden by signing for $2,466,667. On February 15 Roger Clemens of the Boston Red Sox took the all-time lead with a $7.5 million contract for three years. The very next day Orel Hershiser of the Los Angeles Dodgers signed a three-year contract for $7.9 million plus a signing bonus of $1.1 million. Using one third of his bonus for 1989, his year's pay added up to $3,166,667.

In addition, baseball pays excellent fringe benefits in the form of insurance, disability income, and pensions. And players are paid large amounts for endorsing various products. One agent claims that an MVP or Cy Young Award winner should collect up to a million dollars in added commercal benefits. With new television contracts, baseball will receive half its income from TV. And the power of the players' union will mean huge increases in the future.

Baseball requires a variety of skills. You do not have to be especially tall or heavy, and it is possible to be a pro without being exceptionally talented in any one area if you are good in all. You can be a pitcher if you can throw hard with accuracy, and you need not be a good hitter or fielder. If you are exceptionally quick and agile with hands that can fasten onto a fast, hopping baseball and you have a good throwing arm, you have a chance without being a talented hitter. If you have the natural hand-eye coordination necessary to hit a fast, curving baseball you can probably fit in somewhere, even as a designated hitter. It helps if you can run fast, throw hard and straight, and field well, but a natural hitter is the most sought after and highest paid.

In 1988 designated hitters were highest paid ($927,276), followed by first basemen ($785,599) and outfielders ($722,898). The team you play for also makes a difference: The New York Yankees averaged $718,670, while the Chicago White Sox averaged only $226,392.

In addition to those huge salaries in the major leagues, baseball has seventeen minor leagues where most players play for a year or more before making the majors. Most of the minor-league teams are farm teams belonging to one of the twenty-six major-league clubs. If you are signed to a contract you will probably be assigned to one of the minor-league teams until you prove yourself a big leaguer. Salaries of minor leaguers can be anywhere from $850 a month in Class A on up to a major-league figure, since some big leaguers are "sent down" while injured or working out problems. And usually a youngster who was paid a huge bonus to sign will not receive the minimum salary.

Japan allows twenty-four foreigners to play on their twelve teams. Brian Dayett earned less than $62,000 in 1987 as a part-time Chicago Cub. He signed a contract with a Japanese team for $3.7 million over four years. But Dayett says, "It's tough playing away from family and friends. There is the language problem, and the culture is so very different." Bob Horner, a genuine major-league home run hitter, received $2.4 million to play the 1987 season for a Tokyo team, but he refused a three-year contract for $10 million because of the culture difference. Farther down the scale, many AAA players play in the Caribbean winter league and receive $3,000 to $4,000 a month while honing their skills.

Baseball conducts two drafts each year. They usually draft two or three hundred players from high school, from college players who have completed their eligibility, or from free agents. If you are drafted but not signed to a contract within six months, you become a free agent. All players who are not drafted are also free agents. If you are a free agent, you can try out with any team willing to give you a chance. In 1987 the Kansas City Royals alone held 132 tryout camps for 50 to 200 players in each camp. Royals' scouting director Art Stewart said, "At least twelve major leaguers have come out of our camps."

A high school draftee could choose college and thus gain experience plus a degree while waiting to develop into a major leaguer. Since baseball has the most extensive minor-league system of any sport, a good player has ample opportunity to prove his worth. In addition to organized baseball, there are many semiprofessional teams open to anybody who can play well enough, including high school and college players and any other free agents. Major-league teams have scouts all over the country looking for talented players. Therefore, wherever you play, if you are good enough you will be "discovered," especially if someone tips off a scout. You might help your own cause by getting your coach or manager or a sportswriter to contact a scout.

BASKETBALL: Figures from the Detroit *Free Press* show twenty-five basketball players earning over one million for the 1987–88 season, with Patrick Ewing at $2.75 million Their figures show an average salary of about $600,000. The minimum salary, paid to any player good enough to make an NBA team's roster, is $100,000. SPORT estimates that Michael Jordan's endorsements pay him around $3.5 million a year.

Basketball requires quickness and agility and remarkable accuracy in shooting. You also need a quickness of mind to see opportunities in a split second plus a desire to cooperate with other players for the betterment of the team. If you have all this and are exceptionally tall, give basketball a chance. A few players under six feet have been successful, but they must be near the best in the world at shooting, passing, and dribbling. With the three-point circles (19′9″ for colleges and 23′9″ for the NBA), a great outside shooter has a better chance. A few players have been successful even though slow and relatively awkward, but they are usually seven feet tall. You should also have endurance and be strongly built because the no-contact rules of basketball have been roughly shoved aside. The good pros also spent thousands of hours in practice. Unless you are an exceptional athlete in some of these respects, do not expect more than recreation from your basketball.

The basketball teams draft about 230 players in June or July, although this was expected to increase when two new teams were added in 1989. College players must complete their college eligibility before being drafted unless they ask to be drafted. If they ask, they lose their remaining college eligibility. Only fifty or fewer new players make the rosters each year. Thus, hundreds of good players are left out. Since it is a fact that some players improve more than others after college, it is certain that some of these left-out players would become good enough for the NBA if they continued to play.

If you are one of them, what chance do you have? The newly opened Continental Basketball Association offers the best chance. Many Americans play pro basketball in Italy. During the 1987 season Bob McAdoo, who played for the Los Angeles Lakers for fourteen years, led the Milan team to the Italian championship, scoring 29 points. There are basketball summer camps where some excellent players compete. As a long shot, you might try to make the Olympic basketball team and show off your improved talents in the Olympics. Your best hope for the NBA is to improve over the summer and try out as a free agent for next year.

Women's professional basketball has not yet become popular in the United States. The Womens Professional Basketball League folded in 1981 despite paying their players only $8,000 to $10,000. In 1985 the Womens American Basketball Association tried it, but three teams dropped out the first year. In Europe a common salary for women's basketball is reported to be $30,000.

FOOTBALL: The National Football League has more total players—1,372—averaging about $250,000 a year, although a few football players are in the million-dollar-a-year class.

Only four football players made the 1987 SPORT 100, but in

1986 Steve Young, then of the Tampa Bay Buccaneers, was credited with an income of more than $3 million. Young's complicated earnings included $380,000 in salary, $150,000 as a reporting bonus, $1,875,000 of his signing bonus, and $1,275,000 as a contribution to an annuity program. Subtract from his U.S. Football League money the million dollars he paid to buy out his contract, and add $200,000 in salary and the $190,333 prorated share of his signing bonus. The 1987 leader, Bo Jackson of the Los Angeles Raiders, also received multiple incomes totaling $1,391,750 without counting his $383,000 baseball salary and $150,000 bonus.

Gene Upshaw, president of the NFL Players Association, explained why football players are paid less. "Free agency doesn't work. The owners aren't going to bid for players. Why should a guy go out and increase his payroll? He's not going to make any more money." The reason is because, through 1987, each NFL team received about $14 million as its share of television income. That will continue even if the quality of players drops off. Upshaw also complains that the football career is too short. "Ours is just over three years."

Football requires a variety of qualities. All players should be rugged enough, physically and mentally, to survive strenuous contact, and they must be able to put the success of the team ahead of all other goals. Coaches look for speed at all positions, and height and weight are expected to be greater than for most other sports. Linemen need exceptional strength, both natural and acquired. Running backs, wide receivers, and defensive backs need great speed coupled with unusual agility in changing direction. Linebackers need as much as possible of the lineman's strength and the defensive back's speed. A quarterback needs a good throwing arm and exceptional accuracy plus the split vision of a basketball playmaker, a quickness in scrambling away from tacklers, and a presence of mind greater than any other athlete. Other special qualities may win you a pro contract as a punter or a placekicker.

After the fall and winter bowl games, the NFL teams draft 336 players in twelve rounds. The top draft choices receive large sums of money for signing, but only half of the draftees ever make a team. A few remain ready to be activated if one of the regular players is injured, but the others, along with about 1,200 good players who were not drafted, become free agents. They may try out for any team, and the training camps in late summer include many free agents. A few are actually signed to a contract. Most, however, cannot make an NFL team, and there are no minor leagues where players can progress. Some of those play in the Canadian league, where a good player can earn more than $100,000 a year. But linebacker Reggie Williams said, "Going to the Canadian Football League is identity suicide." If you do not play in the NFL or Canada, you can only keep in shape, perhaps by playing on a semipro team, and try again later. Ocasionally, when a team loses a player to injuries, they sign a free agent in midseason.

HOCKEY: Although Wayne Gretzky is now near the million-dollar class, only a handful of hockey players are paid the average baseball salary. The 420 players in the National Hockcy League earn an average of over $200,000. There are several minor leagues where players may earn $30,000 to $40,000 for their six-month season. Hockey is played in Europe, particularly in Austria, Switzerland, and Germany. Some U.S. players earn good salaries there, although the teams limit the number of foreign players.

A hockey player must be a team player even more than a basketball player. Instead of speed, he needs skating ability. He must spend thousands of hours learning to handle the puck with his hockey stick while skating fast. Other than those differences, he needs the same quickness, agility, endurance, and accuracy as a basketball player, but height is not important. A goalie can forgo some of those talents, but he must be exceptionally quick and rugged. Today's hockey players concentrate more on offense and less on defense; therefore, you can help your cause by learning defense.

Young hockey prospects must first learn to skate well. At the age of nine they can begin playing age-group hockey in the youngest of the four age groups, 9–10. The determining factor for learning hockey is the amount of playing time available. In Canada and a small part of the United States, winters are cold enough to freeze ponds or outdoor rinks and hockey is played all winter. Although two hockey players have come from San Diego, ice rinks are rare enough in most areas to all but prohibit hockey. A young player can develop well by playing the equivalent of thirty to forty games a year. Only a few high schools in the U.S. provide this opportunity.

Tom Barrasso did it the Canadian way and found a way to play about 100 games a year. He went directly to the Minnesota North Stars from high school in Massachusetts and won a first-team NHL all-star berth in his first season. A few other U.S. schoolboys have made the NHL immediately, but it is rare, and many experts believe it is wiser to play more before signing. The Pro Elite Draft Development League in Hingham, Massachusetts, prepares young players for the NHL with a ten-week summer season against minor pros and a few NHL players.

The National Hockey League's July draft is like those in other team sports, but the rules are a little different. If you are drafted out of high school and want to go on to college, your team retains draft rights to you until six months after your college career. You can play minor-league hockey instead of going to college, but why not take the college education and four years of hockey competition while you are maturing? After all, it takes a Wayne Gretzky to make the NHL at the age of seventeen, and very few have made it right out of high school.

Good Canadian hockey players usually go into Canadian Junior A leagues. These leagues are like minor leagues, with overnight trips to play in other cities. The players are paid only their expenses, even though they live like minor professionals. Their goal is to make the NHL, and many do. A good American hockey player can choose to play there, and about 5 percent to 8 percent of the players are American. However, Syd DeRoner, former age-group coach, says, "An American boy loses nothing if he goes to a good hockey school in the United States." This is because American college hockey has improved greatly in the past twenty years.

Although your chances in hockey are limited mostly to cold climates, once you learn the game you have ample opportunity to prove your worth, in college or the minor leagues.

SOCCER: There is no set path to professionalism for the good soccer amateur. In the United States the North American Soccer League "died of fiscal exhaustion" in 1985. The Major Indoor Soccer League lost four teams after its season ended in 1988 and planned to continue with seven teams. All this in spite of soccer's being the world's most popular sport, with 55 million players in 155 countries and millions of young people playing in the United States. Dick Berg, general manager of San Jose's defunct team, said, "If people watch soccer on television now, they'll be bored silly." CBS dropped soccer from television coverage on two separate occasions.

The great Italian player Giorgio Chinaglia left his $200,000 a year contract in Italy to play for the New York Cosmos, only to see American pro soccer fail. A great American soccer player might earn high pay in Europe, but for now he cannot earn a living in the United States.

Success at soccer requires some running speed, good endurance, and exceptional skill in directing the ball, both with feet and head. Team cooperation is absolutely essential, and it helps to have a little of the football quarterback's presence of mind because the situation changes rapidly while you have the ball. A goalie must be quick and agile and rugged in diving for the ball. Height is not important, and you will run off any excess weight.

If you are a superstar by American standards you are allowed to play for an international team, but the competition is fierce. The first American to break into the highest level of international pro soccer was two-time UCLA All-American Paul Caligari, who signed in West Germany in 1987.

A semiprofessional league, called the American Indoor Soccer Association, pays its players about $2,500 a month for the five-month season.

The largest and oldest pro soccer league is the English Football League, with 92 teams. With so many foreign teams successful and with thousands of high school teams in the United States, pro soccer should be successful, but perhaps there are too many other pro sports in competition. One ray of hope for soccer players is the expected stirring of interest when the World Cup is played in the United States in 1992.

Individual Sports

GOLF: Inflation of golf winnings continues each year. Here are some official money winnings on the 1988 PGA tour:

1st	Curtis Strange	$1,147,644
10th	Lanny Wadkins	616,596
50th	Corey Pavin	216,768
100th	David Canipe	114,180
130th	Rick Fehr	79,080

In addition to those U.S. winnings, foreign golfers won nearly as much. At about the same time Curtis Strange went over $1 million in November 1988, Ian Woosnam was credited with $1,739,268 from foreign tournaments. Some of the over-fifty seniors can win more money in one year than they won during an entire career when they were in their prime.

A good golfer can be old or young, tall or short, fat or thin, and relatively unathletic. To be great in golf you must be exceptionally accurate. Quickness helps by enabling you to swing faster and thus hit longer shots. Other than quickness and accuracy, you need great mind control, which will let you practice by the hour and avoid choking during competition. You also need maturity and self-control to stand the constant travel and competition on ever-changing golf courses. Gary McCord, pro and TV commentator, says, "The tour can beat you up." Tommy Aaron said, "Golf is mostly a game of failures." And Gary Player said, "When you play for fun, it's fun. But when you play golf for a living, it's a game of sorrows. You're never happy."

To have a chance to play in professional tournaments, you must qualify. To play in the U.S. Open, you must compete in qualifying tournaments. To play on the PGA tour, you must qualify in a series of tournaments that culminate with the Qualifying School. In 1988 the top 52 players in the qualifying tournament received their tour cards. They joined the top 130 money winners and a few exempted former champions on tour in 1989. You must also satisfy other PGA requirements, including experience and financial stability. For information about becoming an Approved Tournament Player, contact the PGA Tour Office.

If you are not good enough to play on the tour, you may play in foreign tournaments until your game improves. At times in the United States, changing each year, a "minitour" has provided nontouring players with pro tournaments. Although the prize money is about 10 percent of that on the PGA tour, some golfers have won a living wage and progressed to the big tour. A new tour, to be called the Ben Hogan tour, is scheduled to start in 1990. Designed for players not on the PGA tour or the Senior tour, there are to be thirty tournaments each year with $100,000 in prize money for each tournament.

Unlike most sports, golf provides an opportunity for you to play professionally all your life. Many golfers over forty win on the PGA tour. When they are fifty they can play on the Senior tour. Most of the leading money winners on the Senior tour win more money than they won on the PGA tour. Here are the leading money winners for 1988 for the over-fifty golfers:

1st	Bob Charles	$533,829
10th	Chi Chi Rodriguez	313,940
25th	George Lanning	129,609

More women have high earnings in golf than in any other sport. Here are some 1988 winnings in the Ladies' PGA:

1st	Sherri Turner	$350,851
10th	Juli Inkster	235,344
50th	Janet Coles	63,465

In 1987 four women won more than Turner's total, with Betsy King leading at $504,535.

TENNIS: For some reason, perhaps because television cameras can cover the entire court, tennis has become a gold mine for professionals, both men and women. Men's professional tennis alone collects around $400 million each year from prize money, television rights, endorsements, and other income. The bad news is that most of the money goes to a limited number of players. Unlike golf, for example, where dozens of players have a chance to win, tennis is dominated by a very few players. Here are the lists for 1986:

Men

Ivan Lendl	$1,963,320
John McEnroe	$1,455,610
Mats Wilander	$1,074,938
Stefan Edberg	$ 729,401
Boris Becker	$ 617,998

Women

Martina Navratilova	$1,328,829
Chris Evert	$ 972,782
Hana Mandlikova	$ 574,849
Helena Sukova	$ 422,387
Pam Shriver	$ 419,686

Martina Navratilova had career earnings of $13,341,712 by mid-1988, while Ivan Lendl had won $12,648,060. Lendl won over $2 million in 1987, and three other men won more than a million. Steffi Graf won $1,063,785 that year, while three other women won more than $700,000.

These players earn their huge sums by playing a grueling schedule the year round. Most of the top players are injured during any given year. Ivan Lendl said, "There is too much play, too much stress, and that is what is causing the injuries." The Association of Tennis Professionals managed to wrest control of the tournament schedule from the Men's International Professional Tennis Council in 1989. The new tour will have 77 tournaments with prize money totaling $38 million. All but three of the top twenty-five players have signed with the new ATP. The international tour will include Moscow and Beijing.

Tennis requires quickness, agility, and considerable accuracy as well as some endurance and a little strength. With those qualifications and thousands of hours of practice, you can play well, but to win you must have a special kind of adaptiveness. Each shot requires you to move into position sometimes in an instant. Faster than you have time to think, you must make a decision as to how to hit the ball. Your shot selection is based upon your difficulty in reaching a position, the position of your opponent, the percentage of success you are capable of for each potential shot, and the percentage of success your opponent will have if you hit that shot. Thus, you need a mind like a computer, programmed by training and by constant monitoring between points.

To break into this highly lucrative profession is fairly straightforward. You merely play in tournaments, working your way up through the age-group rankings and into school and college competition until you are good enough to win some matches in national tournaments. Your next step is the satellite circuit, something of a minor league, where you can win little money but you can begin to win points toward your international ranking. One point will rank you about 1,500 in the world. Winning a satellite circuit will gain 25 to 35 points, enough to rank you in the 300s. If you do well on the satellite circuit, you can move up to the challenger events, which award prize money of $25,000 to $75,000 plus about 30 points for winning one tournament. Only 128 players are good enough to compete at Wimbledon, 16 of them from a qualifying tournament the week before.

The catch, in tennis, is lack of opportunity. A budding tennis player needs a court, fairly expensive equipment, and a good teacher, to say nothing of long hours of practice. This has had the effect of eliminating a large percentage of good athletes, especially those from the inner cities. If your parents belong to a tennis club and encourage you with lessons, it is up to nothing more than your ability and desire. But if you are an inner-city kid who loves basketball but can't expect to beat out all but 300 of the greatest players in the country, what can you do to learn a game that offers greater opportunity? With a little effort you can find a public recreation program to get you started. Then start playing. If you show some talent, you'll be able to find somebody to help you. It's as easy as that, but you must take the initiative yourself. It is not as easy as joining a basketball shootout in a schoolyard.

BOXING: The largest winnings in sports go to the few boxers at the top. In 1988 Mike Tyson knocked out Michael Spinks in 1 minute 31 seconds of the first round. Tyson's prize for that short fight amounted to more than $21 million, and Spinks received $13.5 million for losing!

In these days of inflation, many boxers receive multimillion-dollar prizes. In 1986 Larry Holmes collected $6,625,000 for three fights, and Marvelous Marvin Hagler defeated Thomas Hearns in a fight for which both were paid $5 million. In addition to the prize money, Hagler collected $2.8 million from TV receipts and Hearns received $1.26 million. In 1987 Hagler received $15 million while losing to Ray Leonard, whose pay was $10.8 million.

At the other end of the pro scale, there are boxers taking severe beatings while failing to earn a living. Former middle-weight champion Rocky Graziano said, "Fighting is the only racket where you're almost guaranteed to end up as a bum." And the general atmosphere of boxing is somewhat less than glamorous. Ed "Too Tall" Jones, a great football lineman who tried boxing, said, "I have never been around so many crummy people in all my days."

A good boxer must be even better than a tennis player in adapting to a changing situation. He must be as rugged, mentally and physically, as a football linebacker. He should be as quick and agile as a basketball player, and he needs the endurance of a middle-distance runner. He needs the strength of a shot-putter for a knockout punch. His size makes little difference because of the weight divisions. He must be willing to risk brain damage.

Although it is difficult to work up to the multimillion-dollar payoffs, it is relatively easy to try. Your route is through the amateur ranks, working up through Golden Gloves tournaments and possibly the Olympic Games.

When you decide to turn pro, your main effort should be to obtain a capable and honest manager. Many boxers have lost most of their winnings to crooked handlers. Joe Louis, one of the greatest ever, lived in poverty. His handlers did not leave him enough money to pay his taxes.

BOWLING: Television has made bowling profitable to a select group of professionals through the annual sixteen-week PBA series. Leading money winner of the Professional Bowling Association for 1988 was Brian Voss of Seattle with $225,485, and he won $72,915 in the first seven weeks of 1989. Dave Ferraro of Kingston, New York, won the first prize of $23,000 in the PBA Touring Players Championship, to finish fourth on the money list with $150,395. Voss finished fourth in that tournament to collect $6,500. Not included in the money list are bonuses such as Bob Benoit's $100,000 for rolling a perfect 300. The players bowled for a total of about $4 million in prize money. In 1989 Pete Weber became the fourth man to win over a million dollars in a career.

The Ladies Pro Bowlers Tour scheduled twenty-six tournaments for 1989 with prizes ranging from $30,000 to $200,000. With expenses estimated at $700 per tournament, you must place in the top twenty-four to break even, not counting travel expenses. The LPBT also has regional tournaments where you can experience professional competition on your way up.

Bowling is a game of accuracy, with only moderate strength and endurance needed in addition. Your greatest need, if you are sufficiently accurate, is an opportunity to use a lane and the willingness to practice for thousands of hours.

Bowling is one of the easiest sports to break into. All you have to do is be good enough to roll a high average in one of the thousands of leagues. Your hardest problem will come at the beginning because you need expensive bowling alleys, much time to practice, and good instruction. As an amateur bowler you will join the American Bowling Congress. The ABC has about 5 million members. Your scores will be recorded, and you will have an official average. To join the PBA and become eligible to compete in pro tournaments, a man must have an official average of 190 and a woman must average 175.

Competing in pro tournaments is costly, since you need expenses for traveling and living. Only a few bowlers are good enough to make a living at it, although many more make the effort. The Ladies Professional Bowlers Tour has about 200 competitors. Robin Romeo won $5,000 while winning her eighth tournament early in 1989.

HORSE RACING: Money follows the racehorses to more than 100 tracks in the U.S., and so the demand for jockeys is higher than for players in most other sports. There are about 2,200 qualified jockeys in the United States.

A top jockey might be paid $25,000 for a first-call contract, $10,000 for second call, and $5,000 for third call. If not called by a trainer who has you under contract, you are free to ride for any other trainer. You will receive $25 to $50 per ride plus 10 percent of the purse if you win and 5 percent for second or third. (The wining horse gets 55 to 60 percent of the total purse, with 20 to 22 percent for second and 12 to 15 percent for third.)

By early 1989, to be his final season, Willie Shoemaker had won 8,789 races, more than any jockey in history. He won total purses of over $100 million, and he is still riding in 1989 at the age of fifty-seven. Johnny Longden rode 6,032 winners to the age of fifty-seven. Several jockeys earn more than a million dollars a year, but it can be rigorous work. Lafitt Pincay, Jr., top money winner of the late '70s and early '80s, rode a helicopter between tracks in California so that he could ride in day-night "doubleheaders."

Your size is one of the most important requirements, since horses carry a specified weight in a race. Shoemaker is 4'11" tall and weights 95 pounds. Danny Winnick, at 5'2" and 100 pounds, decided to try to be a jockey when he finished high school even though he had never ridden a horse. He learned in three years. Women have a natural advantage in size and began competing with men in 1968. If your natural weight is around 100 pounds, you need only some strength, a lot of courage, good balance, and quick reflexes, and you must develop excellent judgment of pace and racing tactics. Most of your practice must come from actual riding in races, but it would certainly help to be an experienced rider before you try to race.

Jockey Patrick Day points out another qualification for a winning jockey: "A racehorse is a hypersensitive animal. He can sense if a jockey isn't feeling well, is upset or scared. The hands and reins the jockey uses on a horse are like a telephone people use to communicate. It's a very delicate situation between jock and horse. A rider's attitude has a lot to do with the way a horse runs."

If you are small enough to be a jockey you may work up to a chance to ride by working around the stables. After you learn to care for horses, a trainer may let you begin as an exercise rider. After a year of "riding works" (daily morning rides), you can apply for an apprentice license if you are eighteen years old and have ridden two races under the eyes of the track stewards. An apprentice can be a licensed free-lance apprentice or a contract apprentice. Under a contract you are restricted to riding for one stable but you will receive better all-round training. A free-lancer's certificate allows you to ride for any trainer. Apprentices are sometimes preferred because they receive a lighter weight allowance. You must ride thirty-five winners before you receive your journeyman's license.

HARNESS RACING: The U.S. Trotting Association does not publicize earnings of harness drivers, but many drivers each year ride behind horses that collect over a million dollars in prize money. At 10 percent for the driver, many of them are well paid. Bill Haughton drove horses to purses of more than $40 million during his forty-year career. John Campbell won his percentage of purses totaling $10,186,495 in 1987, and Bill O'Donnell drove to $10,207,372 in prize money in 1985. Prize money has increased dramatically since Campbell topped the list with $3.7 million in 1980.

Mack Lobell, one of the greatest trotters ever to pull a sulky, won $523,150 in one race, a good payoff for the driver. Nihilator had won twenty-four out of twenty-six races as a three-year-old in 1985 for total purses of over $2.3 million.

You can be a harness driver of any age, sex, or size. You must learn how to handle horses, proper pace, and tactics. If sprinting is 90 percent natural talent and 10 percent acquired skills, harness racing is probably just the opposite.

You must work your way up to become one of the drivers who make a good living. Most drivers began as stable boys and assistants to trainers, gradually working up to the opportunity to drive at the matinee meetings. There they can earn a license. Champion driver Bill Haughton says, "I do not know a prominent driver today who was not an expert with a rub rag long before he learned how to handle a whip." The average driver is around forty years old.

You must be at least sixteen years old for a county fair license and eighteen for a raceway license. You do not have to be as light as a jockey. Drivers have won big races in their seventies, and there are some excellent women drivers. Bea Farber's career winnings reached $1.5 million in 1979.

AUTO RACING: Most drivers are paid secret retainers rumored to approach a million dollars. You know the pay is high when you note that the purse for the 1988 Indianapolis 500 alone was $5,000,016.

Many drivers are needed to drive in the Grand Prix, Indy-type, stock car, sport car, drag, and midget racing. Prize money runs into many millions, much of it from advertising money. The driver retains about 30 to 50 percent of his winnings.

Driving a race car requires quick reflexes improved by practicing. It requires courage, because death is always a possibility. It requires great concentration. Bobby Allison said, "The margin of error is very, very narrow." It requires some strength and endurance to handle a car at such speeds for hours. And it requires good eyesight and keen judgment to grasp new situations at top speed. It takes years to develop full skills as a race driver.

Competition in race cars is more complicated than in most

sports because of the many types of events and the many organizations that sponsor races. To begin to understand the setup you need to know the meaning of USAC, CART, NAS-CAR, SCCA, IMSA, NARA, and IHRA.

USAC, the United States Auto Club, sponsors the Indianapolis 500 and other Indy-type races, as well as having a program where you can work up with stock cars, midgets, and sprints. To become a member you must be twenty-one and qualify in experience.

CART, Championship Auto Racing Teams, has only a few hundred exclusive members, but it challenges USAC by sanctioning some Indy-type races.

NASCAR, the National Association for Stock Car Racing, sponsors close to two thousand races on almost 100 tracks for standard production-line cars.

SCCA, the Sports Car Club of America, sponsors amateur and professional racing in many types of road races. Thousands of members race in all the classes of races for a wide variety of cars.

IMSA, the International Motor Sports Associations, has a small membership made up solely of active participants, but it sponsors the Camel GT series in competition with SCCA, and it also sponsors a series of races for low-cost cars.

NARA, the North American Rally Association, also challenges SCCA by sponsoring road rallies.

IHRA, the International Hot Rod Association, sponsors more than a dozen kinds of drag races.

Income for drivers is also complicated, since drivers are paid in many ways. SPORT credited NASCAR champion Dale Earnhardt with $1,699,621.50 for 1987, gained in this way: His eleven victories won $1,154,125. His driving championship earned a bonus of $915,118. He received $30,000 for being Driver of the Year. This total of $2,099,243 was split 50–50 with the owner of his racing car, leaving him $1,049,621.50. Drivers are paid salaries by the owners and most salaries are kept secret, but Earnhardt's was revealed to be $650,000. In addition, he received many payments, such as $20,000 for a commercial and $10,000 for wearing a patch on his driving suit. Earnhardt's big year boosted him to second place among all-time winners with more than $7 million. Only Darrel Waltrip, who won $873,118 as far back as 1982, was ahead of him in NASCAR winnings through 1988.

Income varies between types of races and for each individual. IMSA drivers are paid retainers of about $150,000 for a top driver and $45,000 for a rising star. Formula Atlantic drivers are not paid retainers; their income is from personal sponsors and prize money. The Winston Drag Racing series awards $18 million in prizes for nineteen races.

A few drivers own their own car and collect both ways. But car ownership is not always profitable. It costs $40,000 an hour to run a NASCAR stock car and something like $269,000 an hour to race a Formula One car. Only since large corporations have begun to put money into racing for advertising purposes has auto racing become so profitable.

Some beginners also own their own car, obviously much less expensive. For many would-be drivers, car ownership is the only opportunity they have to race. The most difficult part of working up to the big-money races is to find somebody who will let you drive a car. Unless you can finance the car expenses yourself, your chance of finding a car has a catch: You won't be given a car to drive until you have some experience and you can't get the experience without a car to drive.

Another obstacle to beginners is the fact that the quality of the car is often more important than the ability of the driver. That means that you cannot make a good showing with your driving skills alone. If you drive your own car, another important qualification would be your ability as a mechanic.

Other qualifications for becoming a race driver are good reflexes and coordination and unusual courage. In a sport where accidents and death are common, you need courage.

Many boys begin with their own car, learning mechanics and fast driving, many times unlawfully. An even better approach might be to volunteer as part of the crew on a racing team. You may be allowed to take a racing car for a warm-up and you will certainly learn. Probably a combination of methods works best—your own car, volunteering on a crew, owning a minimum-level car if you can rake up a few thousand dollars, seeking opportunities to drive for anybody, and studying at one of the more than seventy drivers' schools conducted by the Sports Car Club of America. It is certainly possible to make progress as a driver, because thousands of people have done it, including a few women.

RODEO: More than 1,300 rodeos are held each year with over $15 million in prize money. In the famous Calgary Stampede 475 cowboys competed for half a million dollars in 1987. The Pro Rodeo Championship Association, which sanctions half of the rodeos, plans to turn rodeo into a major sport. They already claim $12 million in corporate sponsorship and 13 millions fans.

All-around rider Lewis Feild won $144,335 in 1987, and four others won more than $100,000. Feild's 1986 winnings of $166,042 is the record for one year.

Some young men seem to be natural riders, with the balance and agility needed to stay on a bucking bronco or a twisting bull. In addition, they need a tough mental attitude, because injuries are frequent and often serious. For bulldogging and steer wrestling they must be strong and quick-acting.

To work up toward your share as a rodeo competitor, you must first learn the skills. If you did not grow up on a horse, you can learn at one of the rodeo schools. You can enter local and regional competition. When you are good enough you can try the national circuit.

If you are good at bronc riding or the other events—bull riding, steer wrestling (bulldogging), calf roping, bareback riding, and team roping—your main obstacle will be injuries. Serious injuries are common, and they are the highest price you will have to pay for success.

Women compete in barrel races around a triangular course. Almost 1,000 women belong to the Professional Women's Rodeo Association. In 1988 total prize money for barrel racing amounted to $1,605,250. About eighty women compete in bareback bronc riding, bull riding, and team and calf roping. About ten rodeos each year are for women only. You must pay for a permit to begin competing.

TRACK AND FIELD: Although not officially a professional sport, track offers substantial monetary return. Few can make half a million dollars or more like Carl Lewis or Edwin Moses, but many make living expenses while they train for a chance at the big prize money, which is beginning to appear. The big marathons commonly offer $50,000 to the winner and sometimes throw in a Mercedes. Bonuses are offered for breaking records. Joan Benoit Samuelson collected over $400,000 after her 1984 Olympic victory without trying for money at all. Newspapers reported that Carl Lewis and Ben Johnson were paid $250,000 each for a match race at 100 meters before the 1988 Olympics.

Track and field requires various kinds of abilities. Sprinters need great natural speed, whereas distance runners need natural endurance and the willingness to train hard. Middle-distance runners need a combination of speed and endurance. Hurdlers must have speed plus agility and a sort of reckless courage. Jumpers need spring and throwers need arm strength and they all need agility. Pole vaulters need speed, strength, agility, and courage. They all need the will to train for years before they know whether or not they have a chance to reach the top.

More than most other sports, track requires you to work up through the amateur ranks. When you are good enough you will find the opportunities for earning appearance money, shoe contracts, endorsements, Grand Prix money, and, for now, prize money only in road races.

Other Sports

RACQUETBALL: Professional competition is not extensive, but Marty Hogan, who won close to 90 percent of his matches, earned about half a million a year in the 1980s.

Racquetball requires much the same talents as tennis, with

perhaps more quickness and agility and a faster computer-like mind to adjust to rapidly changing situations.

Like most of the individual sports, racquetball requires proficiency as an amateur before you can play in professional tournaments.

WRESTLING: Professional wrestling is an entertainment rather than a competitive sport, but it requires athletic development, so you should go through amateur wrestling or football. When you think you are good enough, contact a promoter for your next step. The World Wrestling Federation attracts more than $100 million in ticket sales and $200 million in paraphernalia sales plus many millions from cable TV. The star wrestlers are reported to earn $100,000 to more than $1 million in a year.

In March 1989 the National Wrestling League made its debut in Rosemont, Illinois. Called a league of "real" wrestlers, it hopes to attract fans of legitimate wrestling. Three-time NCAA wrestling champion Jim Zlesky said, "It's great to be wrestling again, and it'll be nice to be paid for it. I hope."

AIR RACING: There are no full-time racing pilots, but the pilots almost all have commercial jobs. Only a few races award prizes, and the airplanes are expensive, leaving little profit to the pilots.

ARCHERY: Many professionals are teachers with little opportunity to compete for money. The pro tour offered total prize money of about $120,000 in 1988. The pros are fully sponsored by manufacturers, who hope to profit from the advertising. Although fewer women compete as pros, it is notable that first prize of $1,500 was the same for men and women in the 1988 PAA Outdoor Championship.

BILLIARDS: Prize money in billiards is relatively small. Some pros play exhibitions or teach, and there is a long history of "hustlers" playing pool for money.

CYCLING: According to Jack W. Simes of the U.S. Professional Cycling Federation, professional cycling is the second-largest sport, next to soccer. He says there are about 1,000 licensed professionals in the world. "They can earn anywhere from a thousand to one million dollars."

Most of the big cycling races are Europe's Grand Prix events.

A few Americans have succeeded in these races, even though the sport is hardly known in the United States. You must progress through the amateur ranks until you are good enough to become a professional. There are no women professionals.

FIGURE SKATING: Professional figure skaters, both men and women, perform in ice shows as entertainers, and some teach the sport. You must progress as an amateur, probably in the winter Olympics, before receiving a contract as a performer.

MOTORCYCLE RACING: Professional motorcycle racing in the U.S. offers many purses, but none of the prizes are large. The sport is more popular in Europe, where about two thirds of the Grand Prix winners are Americans.

Many varied types of races are held: speedway, dirt track, road race, drag, hillclimb, indoor, and motor cross. Most racing in the U.S. is sanctioned by the American Motorcycle Association, so you can progress from amateur to pro in the same organization. With several thousand amateur races each year, your main problem is the expense of a motorcycle. The popular 250 class racing bike costs about $11,000. Superbikes are known to lease for as much as $400,000 per year.

Superbikes are produced by factories to boost their sales, and their riders are sponsored. Private competitors, who cannot compete with such expensive bikes, compete in club events, where the best might win as much as $90,000 in a year.

Your best opportunity for learning is on a minibike. Kenny Roberts, a legend as a rider and now becoming a second legend as a team boss, says "To go faster on a GP bike, you have to brake later, flick harder and get on the gas sooner. A minibike sharpens your timing."

Motorcycle racing is not safe. While he was still competing, Roberts said, "There is a little gear behind your brain, and any time the front wheel of the bike makes a funny slip or the back wheel slides, which is about three times a lap, this little gear tells you that you are falling down. Well, when you're eighteen that gear doesn't even work, but when you're thirty-one or thirty-two it's working so well that you aren't comfortable at the speeds you have to go to win."

POWERBOAT RACING: Only a few professional drivers compete each season in the expensive and dangerous unlimited hydroplane races. Professional outboard racing offers more opportunity, but the cost of boats provides the same difficulties as for auto racing. Amateur competition is conducted by the American Power Boat Association. The APBA sanctions more than 400 races each year for more than 8,000 members.

You need a mind oblivious to danger to be a racer. Gold Cup champion Bill Muncey said, "Anything other than death is a minor injury."

SKIING: If you become good enough at racing down hills to compete well in the winter Olympics you may move on to the pro tour. In 1972 champion Jean-Claude Killy said, "There are no amateurs anymore. To be good, a skier must literally devote from four to six years of his life to the sport. You don't have time for school or a job, and you must travel the world. That's hard to do without compensation."

About 4,000 of the 16,000 ski instructors in the United States work full time during the season. They earn from $1,000 to $4,000 a month for four months.

SNOWMOBILE RACING: On a dozen winter weekends you might enter pro races for prize money. Your main qualification is to be able to afford a snowmobile and the substantial entry fee.

SOFTBALL: Although amateur softball thrives, only a few professionals make a living by exhibition touring, and a women's pro league failed in 1980. The good news is that softball equipment sales amount to about half a billion dollars per year, so there is money available for advertising. Craig Elliot of the Grafton, Ohio, Steeles makes about $100,000 a year in slow pitch softball. He works all week and plays several games each weekend. On a lower level many amateurs play in "bandit" tournaments, where as many as twenty teams put up entry fees of as much as $250 each and play all weekend for a first prize of $1,000.

SURFING: The Association of Surfing Professionals has at least twenty events each year during a season, which lasts almost eleven months. Prize money varies. In 1986 the Op Pro at Huntington Beach, California, drew 55,000 spectators and offered $55,000 in prizes. Surfers collect more money for endorsements, ranging close to $200,000 for a champion. Youngsters of eleven or twelve learn in the same surf used by the top performers, and the best, both male and female, can progress through the amateur ranks.

VOLLEYBALL: Unfortunately, volleyball has failed to do well as a professional sport, although the amateur game is popular and well suited to television. At the moment, a talented high school girl can gain a full college scholarship through volleyball. Major League Volleyball, with women's teams in six cities, had plans to expand to eight or ten in 1990 and hoped to catch on with television, but the league folded in early 1989. These women, playing a better game than the top colleges, were paid $5,000 for the eleven-week season with bonuses up to $20,000.

Although men's volleyball is not professional, good players can play two-man beach volleyball on a twenty-eight-event tour, which paid $1.8 million in prize money for 1988. Most of the money comes from companies that use the game as a marketing tool. Christopher "Sinjin" Smith and his partner, Randy Stoklos, have won about seventy events. For 1988 they each collected about $150,000 in prize money and another $100,000 from endorsements.

WATER SKIING: Although there are a few pro tournaments, most male and female water ski pros earn their living from teaching or water shows. The American Water Ski Association lists about sixty-five water ski schools, with an average of three instructors per school.

JAI ALAI: Florida has become the mecca as a professional sport for the Basques, who begin playing as children. Gambling is the reason for the available money. The many frontons in Florida are open most of the year, with several games each night. Eight two-man teams usually play in one game, with players rotating partners for different games. The players are paid good salaries for the season, and they pick up an extra $50 to $100 as incentive money for placing high in each game.

World Jai Alai promotes an extensive training program for amateurs in Miami, Spain, and France, and a few American players are beginning to succeed. Players need the agility of a tennis player plus great skill in catching and throwing with the cesta.

KARATE: Some tournaments pay small prizes—$100 for division winners and $1,000 for overall champions. Full-contact karate fights are staged as in boxing, with a large purse around $50,000, but usually about $5,000 to $10,000.

Jim Coleman, editor of *Black Belt,* estimates a total of about 200 pro fighters in the U.S. Beginners work up in amateur tournaments and progress from there. Women compete in tournaments, but, says Coleman, "are quite rare in the full-contact arena."

CHESS: At the U.S. Chess Championship in the fall of 1988, Michael Wilder, 26, won the first prize of $6,000. He said, "I'm uncertain whether chess can ever really be marketed in this country." Men and women may play chess and work up through the amateur ranks, but like many minor sports it offers little reward other than the joy of winning.

Agents

One of the most important aspects of breaking into pro sports is getting paid. In some sports an agent can help you sign a better contract and find endorsements and appearance money for you.

You do not need an agent until you are ready to receive money for becoming a professional. In fact, if you make an agreement with an agent while you are still in college you will lose all remaining eligibility.

But after you are drafted an agent can negotiate a better contract for you. Agents also add to your income with advertising contracts, personal appearances, and even investment and tax advice. Agents can find alternative jobs, such as Italian professional basketball, if you cannot catch on with the top pro teams. For such services you will pay 3 to 10 percent to your agent, usually 5 percent. Some people advise paying an agent for one job at a time on a time basis, since you are not ready for all those services at the beginning. Some athletes hire a lawyer for the contract negotiations instead of an agent. Lawyers may charge $100 an hour and so be much cheaper as well as more competent at reading contracts.

You should be extremely wary of agents. Thousands of would-be agents are scrambling for only hundreds of jobs, and many have proved themselves unscrupulous. They have been called "vipers" and "parasites." Jerry Vainisi, former general manager of the Chicago Bears, said, "Many are incompetent, even criminal." Ed King, a San Francisco attorney who specializes in suing agents who defraud athletes, said, "If the worst you can say about one of them is that he is incompetent, that probably puts him among the top 5 percent in the sports business."

Sports agent David Lueddeke pleaded guilty to perjury and obstruction of justice and was sentenced to 26 months in prison and fined $10,000 in April, 1989. Lueddeke was charged with enticing college athletes to sign contracts with him before they finished their college career.

Although professional sports have started to protect athletes from bad agents by certifying a list of acceptable agents, there is no protection for rookies. College stars are pestered by more agents than they were by college recruiters while they were in high school. Agents will offer to handle your negotiations without charge, hoping to sign you to a long contract and cash in on your future paychecks. Some agents have taken a kickback from the negotiating team in return for signing a rookie for a smaller bonus.

Attorney Robert H. Prixin, author of *An Athlete's Guide to Agents*, advises, "Any athlete, before hiring an agent, should ask about the agent's qualifications, ethics, philosophy of representation, approach to dealing with club owners, method of calculating and collecting his fees, attitude toward renegotiation...." Then after you hire an agent, he advises you to "monitor the agent's performance, participate in making crucial decisions, and make sure the agent does not subordinate the player's interests to those of another client."

Others advise you to get a list of an agent's other clients and shop around before you sign. You would also be wise to select from the list of registered agents. Try to find an agent who has time for you, since some are overworked. Never give an agent a power of attorney. Do not sign a long-term contract. The NBA forbids its players to sign a contract with an agent for more than one year at a time. And try to find an agent who will be helpful to you after your playing days are over.

In summary, you can become a pro by finding your best sport and playing it until you are good enough. You may need to exploit yourself to break in, since some sports are less rigidly structured than others. Probably the best advice is: TRY HARD.

Chapter VIII

Managing Your Professional Career

How does managing your professional career differ from managing your amateur career? If you worked extremely hard to make it into pro sports, much of your management will be the same. Many professionals realize their opportunities and learn how much harder it is possible to work, and they continue to improve. Others think they have it made and let down on their efforts, sometimes even losing their career through excesses in having fun. In addition, there are some aspects of management that do not apply to an amateur career. In any case, you can improve your life and your career success by working on each of the following areas:

Physical Conditioning

Years ago baseball players used the winter months to loaf over a fishing pole or behind a hunting gun. They put on weight and lost strength, speed, and endurance. A long career lasted until the age of thirty-five. Now they spend the winter keeping in condition, and age thirty-five is regarded as a peak age rather than the end.

Roger Craig of the San Francisco 49ers started as a fullback with almost no reputation for ball-carrying ability. He is a man possessed during the off season, running and training hard with weights. He became a halfback who led the NFL in total yardage and amazed everybody with his strength, speed, and especially his durability.

You have a choice as an athlete. You can try to get by with no more work than the coach forces upon you, or you can improve your conditioning throughout the year.

In addition to improving your strength, speed, and endurance, you should take care of your health. You should learn proper nutrition, avoidance of anything harmful, and prevention of injuries.

NUTRITION: Some athletes have actually eaten themselves out of a job. The most common way is to put on extra weight, but anything that detracts from your general health must surely detract from your athletic performance.

Good nutrition is a combination of eating food that adds to your health and avoiding food that will harm you sooner or later. You must consume a certain number of calories in order to survive. If many of your calories are in food that is bad for you, you suffer in two ways: You harm your body with the bad food and you don't have room for all the good food you need.

The most important thing to learn about nutrition, then, is which foods are good for you and which are bad. Then, if you are serious about taking care of your body, you can begin to cut down on the bad foods and replace them with good.

Nutritionists generally agree on most of the bad foods: fat, sugar, salt, preservatives, greasy fried foods, and any foods that bring on allergic reactions.

If you eat 44 percent of your calories in the form of fats, you are an average American and you are in danger from cancer and cardiovascular problems such as heart attack and stroke. You may find it difficult to reduce your fat intake to 10 percent, but if you are serious you will eat no more than 20 percent. You can reduce fat by avoiding red meat, butter, ice cream, and food cooked in oil. Use nonfat milk, nonfat yogurt, and nonfat cheese.

Sugar is good for you in its natural form—carbohydrates—

but refined sugar is no more than concentrated calories without any additional food value. Dr. Sheldon Reiser of Washington, D.C., has done research showing that 20 percent of the adult population is at risk of suffering heart disease from excess sugar. Since sugar is so concentrated, you can obtain a large percentage of your calories from refined sugar and have no room for the good foods you need. Most people do not realize how much sugar is found in common foods. The worst culprits are desserts, soft drinks, sugared cereals, and the sugar added to tea and coffee. One soft drink may contain six teaspoons of sugar or 120 calories. You could literally starve to death without losing weight if you consumed nothing each day but twenty soft drinks. Excess sugar can also trigger an insulin reaction, something to avoid if your ancestors had diabetes, and also something that can lead to the weak feeling of low blood sugar. You cannot be a good athlete with low blood sugar.

You need some sodium—salt—in your diet, but you can obtain more than enough in the food you eat. Excess sodium is related to high blood pressure. The quickest way to start reducing your sodium intake is to stop adding salt to your food. After a few months your taste will change and you will be happy with the natural taste of foods.

The good foods are those that supply you with a large amount of minerals, vitamins, and fiber plus enough protein and the essential fatty acids. In general, you can be sure you are eating for value when you eat fruits, vegetables, grains, and seeds (which include beans and nuts). Your best protein choice is probably fish. Don't make the old mistake of believing that an athlete needs steak to be strong. Many of the strongest animals are vegetarians, including elephants, bulls, and rhinos. Animal proteins are usually found in food containing excess calories and fats. Excessive proteins overwork your kidneys and can interfere with your absorption of minerals. Dr. George L. Blackburn of Boston sets 15 percent of total calories as the upper limit for protein intake.

One possible problem arises from eliminating meat from your diet. Unless you take iron supplements you may have an iron deficiency that can reduce your endurance.

HARM: You can harm yourself in many ways. The most harm done by humans to themselves comes from smoking, drinking, drugs, and other pollution such as asbestos, plus accidents. Common sense will help you avoid about 99 percent of the harm that might come to you.

Mickey Mantle, referring to two of his drinking buddies, said, "If I hadn't met those two at the start of my career, I would have lasted another five years."

INJURIES: Sports injuries are a special kind of harm that you do not choose to avoid by quitting your sport. The sooner you begin to learn the causes of sports injuries, the sooner you will begin to prevent most of them.

First, you should know that injuries can result from a single violent movement or from gradual wear and tear.

You can avoid wear-and-tear injuries by paying attention. If your new shoes allow friction on your heels or toes, don't shrug off the slight burning or pink skin, because over time you will probably develop blisters or calluses. If tennis or pitching makes your elbow sore, study your movement and change enough to avoid the soreness, or something serious will develop. Aching heels can develop into bruises that will sideline you unless you wear heel cups. You should also pay attention to movements that *might* cause trouble. Prevention includes wearing cushioned shoes and avoiding hard sufaces when possible. Don't put up with any continued discomfort, even as slight as chafing. Your trainer cannot help you if you fail to notice that something is wrong. When you have let something go too far and have developed a problem, remember that your first step in healing is to remove the cause.

You can avoid many of the violent injuries by avoiding unnecessary risks, by using protective equipment, and by warming up properly.

Contact injuries cannot always be avoided, but you add to your chances of injury by crashing into the dugout while chasing a foul ball, diving for a passing shot in tennis, or flying into the seats to save an out-of-bounds basketball. Such hustling is spectacular and on rare occasions wins a game, but you should avoid doing it unless an important game is on the line.

Some players prefer to reduce their protective equipment to lighten their load, but you are foolish to do it against the advice of trainers, coaches, and experienced players. And not all protective equipment is good for you. A study of New Mexico high school football players found that those who wore protective braces on their knees had more than twice as many leg injuries as those who did not wear the devices.

A proper warm-up includes stretching all the muscles involved in your sport and enough movement to open the capillaries to your muscles. Give your body time to adjust to the stress of movement.

Your injuries will be treated by your trainer or coach or, in serious injuries, by a doctor. But you can do some things nobody else can do. You can *feel* the injury, and you can judge your body's response. Only you can judge the difference between a serious, sharp injury and a soreness. The soreness will go away after a short rest and a proper warm-up, whereas a serious injury will only become worse. If a trainer is not present to treat a sudden injury, you should stop using the injured part and apply cold to it with ice or a chemical cold kit. The injured part will begin to ache after a few minutes, then turn numb. After a few minutes of numbness, you may remove the cold pack. After three days, you can begin to apply moist heat.

You are also the best judge of when you can return to play. Never, except in the most extreme emergency, should you submit to taping and a painkiller. Pain is a warning signal; using a painkiller for an injury is like turning off the smoke alarm when your house catches on fire.

Skills

You can't become a pro without excellent skills, but you must consider three facts: (1) Almost never can a skill be fully perfected by the age of twenty-three. (2) Almost all skills deteriorate if you do not practice them. (3) New skills add value to any player.

If you think a new pro cannot improve his skills, why do professional golfers, most of them over thirty years old, practice for hours each day? They even practice before and after playing a round of tournament golf. They know that the more times they swing correctly, the more certain they are of swinging correctly during competition, when one poor swing can cost thousands of dollars.

One of the problems with a skill as complex as the golf swing is the fact that you can compete, and compete well, with less than perfection. Many a professional has worked to revamp his swing after discovering some hitch that keeps him from winning. His faulty swing was good enough to get him into the pro tour, but it prevents him from being a winner.

Sometimes a skill is changed without the knowledge of the player. Johnny Miller spent months doing heavy lifting around his home in the Napa Valley. As a consequence, he developed heavy muscles that changed his swing, and he had to work for two or three years to recover. If you work to strengthen muscles used in your skill, practice your skill at the same time to monitor and keep up with the changes.

Worse than failing to improve is letting your skills slip. Can anything be worse than being careless about a skill that might earn hundreds of thousands of dollars? And yet many pros have done exactly that, through carelessness, laziness, or ignorance. Don't let it happen to you.

Add Another Skill

Once you are a pro you may think you have enough skills, but you should think again. If you made it by doing three things well, why won't you be even better if you can do four?

When you reach the pro ranks you'll find it profitable to add new skills. Some young pitchers, even of high school age, can throw so hard that big-league batters fail to hit them. But in the majors it is a rare pitcher who can survive with nothing but a fastball. Whereas they blasted the ball past the batter in college, they now find some of those pitches hit out of the ballpark. Many a big-league pitcher became a winner only after learning a slider, a split-finger fastball, or even a knuckler.

Bob Benoit tried pro bowling for three years and had to give up. At the age of twenty-nine, he quit the tour and moved to a new city. "I needed a new game to win. If I'd stayed home, I'd have bowled with friends, gotten competitve and never improved." He learned a hook instead of a straight ball and returned to the tour. In January 1988 he won a $27,000 first prize in the Quaker State Open and a $100,000 bonus for rolling a perfect 300.

Keep an inventory of your skills. Consider whether a new skill might add to your total ability.

Think

There seem to be three types of professional athletes. The most common type look upon the profession as a good job. They enjoy playing, but they also have a life to live and they have as much fun as possible. This type may be the one who takes up the cocaine habit or the one who is a good family man with a wife and children. They all act as if they have a permanent job.

The other two types regard their job as temporary. One spends much of the free time working toward a future career. Pro sports offer much free time, whether between seasons or on the airplane between games.

The third type studies his sport. If you learned to think about your sport as an amateur, you will probably continue as a pro. Even though you are one of the first two types, you should think during competition and training in order to gain an extra edge over your competition. If you are the third type, you also think during your free time. If you become a full-time thinker you will probably go on to be a coach or manager after you stop playing.

Part of your thinking, of course, is to monitor your progress. The principles are the same as for your amateur career, but some of your goals will be different. For example, one of your goals should be your career after your playing days.

Prepare for your Future

You will want another career after your playing days end. The average professional player needs a job by the age of thirty, but even most of the highly successful players retire by the age of forty. If you were ambitious enough and energetic enough to carve out a professional career, you will not be content with sitting around for the rest of your life.

The time to prepare for that career is while you are in college, but it is never too late. During the few years you are in pro sports you have time to observe life around you and decide what you want to do. Then you will be wise to make some preparations. The preparations may be more study, making contacts with people, and making plans. To motivate yourself, imagine yourself out of the sport with no job and nothing to occupy your time.

Agent

Unless you made the mistake of signing a lifetime contract with an agent, you have the opportunity of choosing a new one whenever you wish. And from your contacts with other players you will have some idea of which agent you want.

Now that you are a pro, your agent is there to negotiate each new contract, to find endorsements that will pay you well, and, if you wish, to find you speaking engagements, sessions at training camps, interviews, even a book deal. If you are famous enough to bring in many such money-making deals, you will want a full-time agent. If you need nothing more than a new contract every two years, you might consider hiring an agent for that specific purpose.

In any case, don't give your agent full authority on your behalf. You don't want to be at home when the rest of the team is in training camp simply because your agent tried too hard to boost your salary. If you would rather sign for $900,000 with the team you've been with for your whole career than receive $1.2 million with a team clear across the country, tell your agent your feelings before he begins. If you don't want to endorse cigarettes or liquor, tell your agent. Giving an agent free rein is like having a conscience transplant. Your agent is supposed to work for you, and you are supposed to be the boss.

Investments

Some of the leading money-makers in pro sports have died penniless. Many other have lost much of their fortune before realizing the importance of saving and investing. When money pours in and you believe it will continue, it is tempting to spend it.

Garry Maddox, former major leaguer, said, "There are two kinds of nouveau riche athletes. Those who spend to make up for everything they never had. And those who want to hold on to every penny."

As soon as you receive more money than you need for living expenses, you should make a plan. Call it a budget if you wish, but make it definite.

First, set aside all you will need to pay your income taxes. That will amount to almost half of it. Second, set aside the amount you will need for living expenses. If your money is a bonus payment, it will not be repeated and you should budget enough for a year's living expenses.

Third, divide the remainder, saving at least half of it. You may think half is too much to save, but after taxes and living expenses a $500,000 bonus is reduced to about $210,000, and your savings of $105,000 are only 21 percent of your bonus. On a bonus of only $100,000 your savings would be only about 10 percent.

Even if you are wise enough to save money, you can lose it through poor investments. There are many ways to invest your savings, but your main goal is to retain all of it. As soon as you have money, people will try to influence your investments. Many will promise returns of 20 percent a year or more, but you should remember that the higher the return, the greater your risk. Unless you are an expert and are willing to spend many hours watching your investment, you should play it safe and allow compound interest to work for you.

Compound interest is amazing. If you reinvest all the interest on your money, it will grow surprisingly. To know how many years it will take to double your money, divide 72 by your rate of interest. Thus, income of 8 percent will double your money in nine years. That means that if you saved $100,000 from your bonus at the age of twenty-three, by the time you reached fifty-nine it would have grown to $1,600,000! You are not likely to match such growth by speculating.

Young athletes are seldom prepared to invest large sums of money. You will be wise to pay a financial adviser to help you. Your agent will probably offer to be your financial adviser, but most agents are not qualified. One agent went to prison for losing $1.2 million for fifty professional players in the 1970s. Another lost $6 million for fourteen athletes, and their losses may reach $15 million after IRS interest and penalties. If you earn at least an average pro salary you will need an agent, a financial adviser, and an accountant. Be wary of combining these jobs in one man.

Marriage and Family

Most young professional athletes do not seem ready for marriage and a family. Their sudden heady riches make them think the world is their oyster, and they sow their wild oats as if they have only a year to live. Just as they fail to save money for the future and ignore the fact that they will be out of a job in a few years, they seem oblivious to what it takes to enjoy the good life in later years.

If you are wise, you will give some mature thought to the time-honored values of family life. If you do, you will sometimes conduct yourself differently. Think about it.

Prepare for a Nonplaying Job

If you like sports, you would like to be a glamorous, highly paid professional athlete, but if you cannot make the grade, or if you do and your career ends, you want another career. If you would like a nonplaying career in sports, your chances are good—several hundred times as good as becoming a professional athlete.

You can be connected with sports as a coach, in sports medicine, in the media, as an official, or in business. In each of those vocations your opportunities are greater if you understand sports from the player's viewpoint, especially if you made a name for yourself as a famous athlete.

Coach

There are more than 158,000 coaches in 19,800 U.S. high schools, more thousands in colleges, and hundreds in pro sports.

Many high school coaches are paid as teachers, with most receiving extra pay or time for coaching. At the other extreme, Bill Walsh reportedly received $1,300,000 for coaching the San Francisco 49ers in 1988. Coaching pay is not always as low as it might appear. In 1979 "Pepper" Rogers of Georgia Tech had an official salary of $42,549, but he had an additional $150,000 of fringe benefits. Helenio Herrera earned $240,000 in 1971 for coaching soccer in Italy.

The head coach of a team is responsible for obtaining the best possible players, training them, devising game tactics, and controlling the game action as much as possible. Assistant coaches are assigned duties to help the head coach. Many high school coaches also teach classes part of the time, especially physical education classes. Coaches of individual sports spend most of their time teaching individual skills and have little to do during the actual competition. To be successful, both at winning and at developing character, a coach should be a teacher and a leader, good at getting along with people and persuading them to follow orders. With the great increase in women's sports, female coaching jobs are multiplying rapidly.

"Coaching has changed," says Jackie Sherrill, who was paid $287,000 a year to coach football at Texas A&M. "Twenty years ago the coach never left the campus. Now I balance the budget, market the product, do promotions, handle personnel, sell the program, recruit, and coach. Like it or not, it's a different type of business now." He made forty trips during 1982 to speak to alumni groups.

Bear Bryant, the winning coach of Alabama football, said, "I've never recommended anybody go into coaching, 'cause if they have enough on the ball, if they can do without coaching, they should do without it. If they put as much work into it and spend as much time, the rewards are going to be much better in something else." Al Conover, former coach at Rice, said, "I'm going to become a hog farmer. After some of the things I've been through, I regard it as a step up." And Alabama basketball coach C.W. Newton said, "When a coach is hired, he's fired. The date just hasn't been filled in yet." Major-league baseball managers are fatalistic about their futures; they average more than five firings per year. Sportswriter Red Smith said, "I can think of three managers who weren't fired. John McGraw of the Giants, who was sick and resigned; Miller Huggins of the Yankees, who died on the job; and Connie Mack of the Athletics, who owned the club."

Other coaches live as dangerously as baseball managers. Basketball coach Bob Zufplatz said, "Sometimes it's frightening when you see a nineteen-year-old kid running down the floor with your paycheck in his mouth." Football coach Lou Holtz said, "A lifetime contract for a coach means if you're ahead in the third quarter and moving the ball, they can't fire you."

The conventional way to become a coach is to take education courses in college, probably specializing in physical education. You need athletic experience, and you should take public speaking to prepare for speaking to your team as well as for many public appearances. It is possible to become a coach in the pro ranks without a college education, but it is rare outside of baseball. Your chances of becoming a coach in the pro leagues are less than your chances of becoming a player, since there are five or six players for each coach and coaching careers last longer. If you aim for a coaching career, be sure you would like it even if you spend your life coaching in high school.

In most sports you must have some success as a high school coach before applying for a college job. And then you need even more success in college to attract attention for a pro job. In baseball, if you learn the game thoroughly and have all the coaching qualifications of leadership, you can follow a playing career with a minor-league coaching job and progress from there.

Bill Walsh's career shows how slowly even such a great coach works up in the ranks. He began as a high school coach and moved up to the university ranks three years later as a defensive coordinator. He changed universities, still an assistant, then became an assistant coach for two pro teams. After eight years with Cincinnati he was passed over for the head coaching job and moved to San Diego as offensive coordinator. After one year he took the head coaching job at Stanford for two years. His good record there won him the job as head coach of the San Francisco 49ers, twenty-two years after he started coaching.

To rise in stature as a coach, heed the words of two of the best football coaches: Vince Lombardi of the Green Bay Packers said, "Coaches who can outline plays on a blackboard are a dime a dozen. The ones who win get inside their players and motivate." Bud Wilkinson of Oklahoma said, "You can motivate players better with kind words than you can with a whip."

Golf Pro

One specialized category of coaching is teaching golf. Since golf is so popular and so much money is spent on playing the game, there is great demand for lessons to improve the game of the nation's amateurs, from hackers to champions.

There are 8,200 PGA golf pros and 4,500 apprentices. About one fourth of the golf pros earn less than $20,000 a year, and only about one fourth earn over $30,000. An assistant pro is paid about $750 a month plus fees from giving lessons.

Thus, the fame and fortune go to the touring pros, but the vast majority are teaching pros. A few teaching pros play a limited amount of tournament golf.

In addition to learning to play golf and teach others to play, you must learn to maintain a golf course and run a business, including salesmanship and public relations. The PGA developed a four-and-a-half-year course at Ferris State College in Michigan where you can major in professional golf management.

To be a good teacher you need tact, enthusiasm, and patience. A golf pro also needs business skills.

The PGA apprentice program takes three to seven years. This includes active work under a Class A pro, formal study in two business schools, and passing the Playing Ability Test and an oral examination.

Sports Medicine

There are a few jobs for professionals who would like to specialize in sports. For example, a physician might specialize in sports medicine or a researcher might concentrate on studies in sports physiology. Exercise physiologists might, instead of working to restore victims of auto accidents, work only with athletes.

By far the most jobs are available to trainers. Almost all colleges and all the pro teams have an athletic trainer. There are about 10,000 trainers in the United States. A certified athletic trainer works in six areas:

1. Prevention of injuries.
2. Recognition and evaluation of injuries.
3. Management, treatment, and disposition of athletic injuries.
4. Rehabilitation.
5. Organization and administration of the training program.
6. Education and counseling of athletes.

To become a trainer you need undergraduate work, many hours of practical work, and graduate work.

You need formal instruction in prevention, evaluation, and emergency care of injuries. You need instructional methods, health, and administration of training programs. You need courses in anatomy, physiology, kinesiology, nutrition, and psychology. Also recommended are chemistry, physics, pharmacology, statistics, and research design.

To enter the graduate program you also need 800 hours of clinical experience under a trainer certified by the National Athletic Trainers Association.

Your graduate work will include advanced study in some of the undergraduate subjects, plus sports law and 400 hours of clinical experience.

To become certified by the NATA, you must have certificates in first aid and CPR and pass the NATA Certification Examination. A teaching certificate enables you to teach and to work as a trainer with extra pay at the beginning.

The NATA has 10,000 members, but it believes that high schools offer the possibility of 10,000 to 20,000 jobs, depending upon how administrators and the public recognize the need for trainers. They estimate one million injuries among the 5.8 million high school athletes each year (636,000 in football, 126,000 in girls' basketball), and yet only 1 in 5,000 high school athletes receives comparable care. They urge athletes and their parents to ask principals, athletic directors, the medical society, and the school board to add trainers.

A trainer's most urgent duty is to give first aid during games or training. Usually a doctor is not present and the trainer substitutes, taking care of routine injuries or illnesses and sending the athlete to a physician for more serious care. A trainer does the bandaging and gives rubdowns. Some trainers become so expert in sports injuries that they can diagnose and cure better than a general physician. For example, a pitcher with a sore arm would be advised to rest by a doctor, but an experienced trainer might have him pitching in a few days. A trainer should help the athletes with preventive health care, both from injuries and from a careless life-style.

If you are not a star athlete and want to be a trainer, you might start as a student manager in high school or college. Your duties could be anything from water boy up to actually assisting the trainer by giving rubdowns. After your college education, you might work as a teacher and part-time trainer. With experience, the teaching duties become fewer as the trainer progresses toward a full-time job at the college or professional level.

Reporter

There are over 24,000 male and 16,000 female reporters in the U.S., working for the 1,762 daily newspapers and the 7,579 weeklies. Probably about 4,000 of these are sportswriters, with some others doing double duty. Some newspapers hire sports photographers. Average starting salary is $10,000 to $31,000. On a morning paper you begin work in late afternoon and work until midnight.

Your job as a sports reporter is to observe and report competition and interview athletes and coaches. On small newspapers you will have extra duties whenever sports reporting is not a full-time occupation. For example, on a newspaper a sports reporter is usually given the task of reading all the sports reports on the wire service and rewriting them according to whatever the newspaper chooses to print.

Being a sportswriter is not all fun and glamour. Red Smith said, "Writing a column is like opening a vein and letting words bleed out, drip by drip." Not all sportswriters are really experts. English sportswriter Cliff Temple wrote, "A journalist is someone who would if he could but he can't, so he tells those who already can how they should." And sportswriters are not always favored by the athletes and coaches. Joe Paterno, the Penn State coach, said, "If I ever need a brain transplant, I want one from a sportswriter, because I'll know it's never been used."

Some reporters work for colleges or the pros to handle publicity for their teams. Most colleges and all pro teams have a Sports Information Director. Small operations hire part-time SIDs.

As SID you will prepare handouts to any newspaper, radio station, or television people likely to report or comment on any of your games, athletes, or coaches.

To be a sports reporter or SID, you must learn to write fluently in order to turn out interesting and understandable reports in a short time. Among your high school subjects, you should take English and typing. All jobs require someone with knowledge of sports, so a background as a competitor certainly helps, but even more important is a keen interest in sports.

If you have that interest in sports and like the idea of being a sports reporter, you can still try to progress as far as possible as a player. At the same time, some of your elective courses should be in journalism. You should take every opportunity to write for the school paper. One of the advantages of a writing career is that you can do it in your spare time. In high school or college you might write a sports interview and attempt to sell it to your local newspaper. Even if you fail, you will have spent your time toward improving yourself.

Announcer

Pay for television sports announcers is startling, as seen in this 1986 list:

Brent Musburger, CBS	$1,900,000
Marv Albert, NBC	$1,700,000
Pat Summerall, CBS	$1,300,000
Vin Scully, NBC	$1,100,000
Al Michaels, ABC	$1,100,000

At the other end of the scale you might start working for a radio station for as little as $100 a week.

Radio and television employ many announcers and commentators, although far fewer than newspaper reporters. On television, sports reporting for two or three minutes on the nightly news is much less than a full-time job.

To be an announcer you should have a pleasant, well-modulated voice, and for television you should also have a pleasing appearance. You should know your sport thoroughly, and it helps to be well educated and have a sense of humor.

To prepare yourself as an announcer, you might follow in the footsteps of Al Michaels. At the age of ten he somehow decided to be an announcer, and he went around announcing everything. He turned down the audio on the television set and announced games as he watched. Following the gardener, he would give a play-by-play report: "He's put down the rake, and now he's grabbed the hose."

Announcing is not as easy as it may appear. Michaels says, "Just getting in front of the camera in front of millions of people is pressure in itself. To take an announcer's comment—one line in an entire broadcast—and then take it out of context and make him look foolish, is ridiculous. I mean, everything's ad-libbed. Johnny Carson is reading off cue cards."

Versatility is helpful when trying to break in, since many small radio stations need someone who can do several jobs. If you have a First Class Radio-Telephone Operator permit, you have an advantage because each station is required to employ one. It will also help if you can write and sell. You should take public speaking in school and do any available radio work. To break in, when you think you have something to offer, you need to apply. You might even do an interview on tape and try to interest your local radio station.

Sportcaster Paul Guanzon offers a little advice on how to break in: "It's not politics, it's just who you know."

Official

A few officials make a living from their work. Most of the thousands of officials, however, are part-time workers on nights or weekends, since most sports need officials for limited duty. Hockey needs eight officials per game, and basketball uses six, including two scorers and two timers. Baseball needs only four per game. Baseball umpires are reported to be the highest paid officials, with the major-league umpires earning about $70,000 per year, basketball officials receiving about $40,000, and hockey officials $30,000, but SPORT listed Earl Strom, NBA referee, at $125,000. Pro football officials are paid $300 to $800 per game.

An official enforces the rules of the game, often making split-second judgments. To be a good official you must know the rules, have the eyesight necessary to observe infractions, and have the impartial mind and courage to make calls against a hostile crowd. An official must be able to stand jeers and anger from the crowd. Referee Strom said, "Officiating is the only occupation in the world where the highest accolade is silence."

Officials also need endurance. It is estimated that NBA referees run six miles per game. The hockey official must skate with thirty rotating players for sixty minutes.

The pro sports teams scout for officials in the same way the teams look for athletes. Therefore, you begin by officiating in amateur sports and hope to work up. When you decide you would like to be an official you should volunteer your services as an unpaid official. Little leagues need umpires, tennis tournaments need linesmen, even some playground games use officials. In sports such as auto racing or horse racing, most officials come from people already involved in the sport. It is possible to step right into a paying job after a sports career, but it is not likely and you'd better be extremely good.

Administration

Behind the players and coaches on the playing field lies an organization necessary to the administration of sport. Somebody must handle the money necessary for preparing the playing field, for uniforms and equipment, the coach's salary, the officials' wages, travel expenses, and tickets. Somebody has to schedule the games, supervise eligibility, sell tickets, and clean the stadium. In the pro ranks, somebody has to hire coaches and sign and trade players.

Colleges large enough to have an athletic program have an athletic director who oversees most of the above duties. Some athletic directors have staff members who handle some of the duties.

As far back as 1982, when all salaries were lower, the median salary for athletic directors in twenty-seven large public universities was $58,300. For fifty-three private universities, the average A.D. received $45,300. But the famous Illinois football coach Bob Zuppke says, "No athletic director holds office longer than two unsuccessful football coaches."

Pro teams have the equivalent of athletic directors. Baseball clubs, for example, have general managers whose most important duties include signing and trading players. The team hires other people to be business manager, ticket director, traveling secretary, and stadium director as well as smaller administrative positions. If you want to apply, experience in a lower-level job is usually a requirement.

If you want to work toward the good salaries of athletic directors, your best method is to work first as a coach. Assistants to the A.D. may work up from lesser jobs and may have a chance to become athletic director.

In addition to college and professional teams, administrators are needed for the various leagues and conferences. Some administrators earn large salaries. Peter Ueberroth went to work as commissioner of major-league baseball at a salary of $450,000. Donald Fehr, executive director of the Major League Baseball Players Association, received $300,000. There is no set path for working up to such jobs. You need experience as a business executive with some connection to sports.

Another rather large field is the administration of public recreation, where a city might hire you to supervise the city's playgrounds and recreational activities. Some physical education majors include study in this specialty. You will probably have to catch on as an assistant and work up or enter the field from a teaching career. Salaries are similar to teaching pay.

Business

A business can be one you own or one where you work. Most businesses sell things or services. The possible range of sports business can range all the way from ownership of a team down to selling programs during a game.

Most sales are for sports equipment. Thousands of sporting goods stores sell shoes, balls, clubs, rackets, clothing, books, and many other items. Some specialize in only one, such as shoes or golf clubs. You should probably begin as a sales clerk and work up until you can start your own business. There is great risk of losing money in business, but a successful business will pay you more than most jobs. Your chances will improve if you study accounting and business administration.

Services can include almost anything, but the most popular services teach fitness and sports skills or furnish a place to play. Fitness can be taught at minimum expense by renting a hall for aerobic dancing, or you can spend a million dollars or more on a well-equipped gymnasium. Skills can be taught without great expense, but you need a thorough knowledge of the sport and of teaching methods. You can be an instructor in anything from karate to chess.

The largest capital investments in sports are for the many places to play. You might own, manage, or work for a golf course, tennis club, bowling alley, swimming pool, or any kind of sports field. The income can be large. The Pebble Beach golf course in California, for example, sends out foursomes at ten-minute intervals until about four hours before dark. They are booked months in advance at a price of $600 per foursome. Ski resorts and tennis camps also charge high fees. Where there is money, there are jobs. More consumer money goes into golf than any other sport. The estimate for 1986 showed $20 billion spent on golf, and tremendous increases are projected because of inflation and because of golf's attraction as a social sport and one that improves business relationships. Gordon Benson of the National Golf Foundation says that 21 million golfers played in the United States in 1988 on 12,000 courses. "The total could reach 40 million by the year 2000." Many small companies are trying to collect some of this money. If you can offer something golfers can use, you can earn some of it for yourself.

Miscellaneous

A few opportunities do not fit into a large category, but one of them might suit your fancy.

How about being a coach of horses? They call them TRAINERS, but they perform the same service for a racehorse as a track coach performs for middle-distance runners. A top trainer earns large sums of money, and if you love horses and competition it is a good life. You must start by working around the stables and by keeping your eyes and ears open while you do menial chores.

A few CADDIES travel the golf tour as full-time professionals. Once in a while, when your golfer wins a big tournament, you might be rewarded with several thousand dollars for your week's work. At other times you might earn little more than expenses. If you like golf that much, you can start caddying at your local golf course.

Professional teams have SCOUTS who travel about the country watching good athletes compete in school and college games. The scout's job is to find athletes who are good enough to be signed by the pro team. You'll need a thorough knowledge of the sport, usually gained by playing for years and, sometimes, by coaching. Scouting is not a job to decide upon while you are in high school; wait until you have a professional career.

Tony Lucadello, scout for the Philadelphia Phillies, commented about the difficulties of scouting: "Unfortunately, too many parents and coaches think winning at an early age is more important than learning. I have seven guys who work for me. As a group, we seen an average of 30,000 players a year. This year we saw four players who had major-league potential, only four."

Many teams, even some college teams, pay a STATISTICIAN to keep records of all their players in competition. A statistician uses those raw numbers to find significant "stats" for the team. For example, when a baseball manager looks down the bench for a pinch hitter in the late innings, he keeps in mind the statistician's figures on how well each hitter has done against right- or left-handed pitchers, against this team, in this ballpark, and even in this particular inning, as well as who has been hitting the best in recent days. A statistician may not be particularly well paid, but some people are so keenly interested that they would do it for nothing, for fun. You must understand your sport, be good with numbers, and know how to use a computer.

The standard way to become a statistician is through college with training in statistics and computer programming. For details on the profession, contact the American Statistical Association (806 15th Street NW, Washington, DC 20005). But to be an *applied* statistician you must know your field, so sports knowledge may be more important in your case. Certainly, your most important asset would be a consuming love of sports statistics. If you keep statistics as a hobby and find some interesting results, you can contact publications or teams that should be interested.

Agent

An agent for professional athletes can earn large sums of money. Professional athletes earn around a billion dollars a year. At 5 percent, agents would receive $50 million a year. The bad news is that, since there is no limit to the number of agents, the average income is much lower than $10,000 a year for the thousands of agents. But since the registered agents represent most of the high-paid athletes, their average income is considerably higher. Unless you can beat out most of the competition or have the inside track to a great athlete, your chances of making a good living as an agent are not good. Jack Mills, one of the better independent agents, represented 414 football clients in twenty years. Some agents have only one client.

Agents wield increasing power in sports. Mark McCormack, head of International Management Group, said, "We're by far the most powerful influence on sport in the world. We could turn any individual sport—golf, tennis, skiing—on its ear tomorrow."

To be an agent, you need no definite educational or professional requirements. The only regulation is registration with the NFL or NBA. Professional baseball is also beginning to require agents to register. Football registered 1,500 agents in 1983 but reduced that number to 700 in 1987. Your best chance to break in is by handling rookies, since you do not have to be a registered agent. You need good personal salesmanship, first to sell yourself to a prospective client, and second to negotiate good contracts for your clients. You also need full knowledge of each sport, especially how much each team might be willing to pay.

The main duties of an agent are negotiating contracts and finding endorsements, but most agents take on other duties ranging from acting as financial manager down to small personal services. (One agent in Boston received a call from Honolulu asking him to get some hot water in the player's bathroom.)

Most players regard agents with favor—when they need them. Former Cincinnati pitcher Tom Seaver said, "In negotiations it's a question of whether you think they are being fair with you or trying to stick it to you. I'd rather be represented by an agent when I feel they are trying to stick it to me."

If you are not a lawyer, your best opportunities to become an athletic agent are to work for a general agency or to be so well known as a former athlete or coach that you can attract young athletes to your stable. As an athlete, you might prepare for being an agent by learning the basics of negotiating through study and practical experience.

If you love sports and are determined to work in that field, there is almost surely a place for you. Perhaps not as one of the highly paid athletes but certainly in a nonplaying job. Many of these jobs are not what you would call routine or standard jobs. Most are unusual, so you cannot enter them by the usual routes of school and employment agency. You have to go to the job and present yourself as somebody who likes to do that work. Somewhere among all those strange and wonderful jobs is something for almost every sports lover.

Appendix

Professional Associations and Books on Sports

You can obtain specific information about your sport from books, from magazines, and from the associations that govern the sport or assist athletes. Most books and magazines are of limited help but they are interesting to anyone in that particular sport. Ask your librarian for lists. Below are some associations and a few publications of particular interest.

Administrator

College Athletic Business Managers Association, Holy Cross College, Worcester, MA 01610.

Air Racing

U.S. Air Racing Association, P.O. Box 60084, Reno, NV 89506.

Announcer

Wolf, Warner. *Gimme A Break!* New York: McGraw-Hill, 1983.

Archery

Professional Archers Association, 7315 North San Anna Drive, Tucson, AZ 85704.

Auto Racing

Sports Car Club of America, 6750 South Emporia, Englewood, CO 80112.

United States Auto Club, 4910 West 16th Street, Indianapolis, IN 46224.

National Association for Stock Car Racing, 1801 Volusia Avenue, Daytona Beach, FL 33015.

International Hot Rod Association, P.O. Box 3029, Bristol, TN 37620.

Baseball

Major League Baseball Players Association, 1370 Avenue of the Americas, New York, NY 10019.

Basketball

National Basketball Players Association, 15 Columbus Circle, New York, NY 10023.

Continental Basketball Association, 425 South Cherry Street, Denver, CO 80222.

Billiards

Billiard Congress of America, 1901 Broadway Street, Suite 110, Iowa City, IA 52240.

Professional Pool Players Association, 422 North Broad Street, Elizabeth, NJ 07206.

Bowling

Ladies Pro Bowling Tour, 7171 Cherryvale Road, Rockford, IL 61112.

Professional Bowlers Association of America, 1720 Merriman Road, Akron, OH 44313.

Bowling, 5301 South 76th Street, Greendale, WI 53129.

Bowlers Journal, 875 North Michigan Avenue, Chicago, IL 60611.

Boxing

Golden Gloves Association of America, 1704 Moon Avenue, Albuquerque, NM 87112.

Coach

Sabcock, Ralph J., PhD. *The Coach*. Philadelphia: W.B. Saunders Co., 1973.

Rooney, John F. *The Recruiting Game.* Lincoln: University of Nebraska Press, 1980.

Scholastic Coach, 50 West 44th Street, New York, NY 10036.

Cycling

U.S. Professional Cycling Federation, R.D.#1, Box 1650, New Tripoli, PA 18066.

Football

NFL Players Association, 1300 Connecticut Avenue NW, Washington, DC 20036.

Canadian Football League, 1919 Scarth Street, Regina, Sask. S4P 2H1.

Golf

PGA, 112 TPC Boulevard, Ponte Vedra, FL 32082.

Ladies PGA, 1250 Shoreline Drive, Sugar Land, TX 77478.

Golf Pro

The Professional Golfers' Association of America, Box 109601, Palm Beach Gardens, FL 33410–9601.

Harness Racing

United States Trotting Association, 750 Michigan Avenue, Columbus, OH 43215.

International Trotting and Pacing Association, 575 Broadway, Hanover, PA 17331.

Hockey

NHL Players Association, 65 Queen Street West, Toronto, ON M5H 2M5.

Hockey News, 2178 1434 Street, Catherine Street West, Montreal, Quebec, Canada.

Horse Racing

Jockey's Guild, Inc., 555 Fifth Avenue, New York, NY 10017.

Jai Alai

Goitia, Jose M. *The Other Side of the Screen,* 1983.

Karate

Black Belt, P.O. Box 7728, Burbank, CA 91510–7728.

Motorcyle Racing

American Motorcyclist Association, P.O. Box 141, Waterville, OH 43081.

Official

National Association of Sports Officials, 1700 North Main Street, Racine, WI 53402.

Gerlach, Larry R. *The Men in Blue*. New York: Viking, 1980.

Referee, Box 161, Franksville, WI 53126.

Powerboat Racing

American Power boat Association, P.O. Box 377, East Detroit, MI 48021.

Racquetball

U.S. Racquetball Association, 1800 Pickwick Avenue, Glenview, IL 60025.

Rodeo

Professional Women's Rodeo Association, 8909 Northeast 25th Street, Spencer, OK 73084.

International Professional Rodeo Association, P.O. Box 615, Pauls Valley, OK 73075.

Prorodeo News, Professional Rodeo Cowboys Association, 101 Prorodeo Drive, Colorado Springs, CO 80919.

S.I.D.

College Sports Information Directors of America, Campus Box 114, Texas A&I Univ., Kingsville, TX 78363.

Soccer

Major Indoor Soccer League, One Bala Cynwyd Plaza, Bala Cynwyd, PA 19004.

Soccer America, Box 23704, Oakland, CA 94623.

Sports (general)

Youth Sports, All-American, 5520 Park Avenue, Trumbull, CT 06611.

Women's Sports Publications Inc., 310 Town & Country Village, Palo Alto, CA 94301.

Young Athlete, 1601 11th Avenue, Bellevue, WA 98004.

Skiing

Professional Ski Instructors of America, 5541 Central Avenue, Boulder, CO 80301.

United States Ski Coaches Association, P.O. Box 100, Pork City, UT 84060.

World Pro Skiing-Racers Association, P.O. Box 4580, Aspen, CO 81611.

Statistician

Friedman, Arthur. *The World of Sports Statistics*. New York: Atheneum, 1978.

Tennis

Association of Tennis Professionals, 319 Country Club Road, Garland, TX 75040.

Track and Field

The Athletic Congress, 155 West Washington Street, Indianapolis, IN 46204.

Trainer

National Athletic Trainers Association, P.O. Box 1865, Greenville, NC 27858.

Training

Nelson, Cordner. *Excelling in Sports/How to Train*. New York: The Rosen Publishing Group, 1985.

Nideffer, Robert M. *Athletes' Guide to Mental Training*. Champaign, IL: Human Kinetics Pub., 1985.

Tutko, Thomas, PhD, and Tosi, Umberto. *Sports Psyching—Playing Your Best Game All of the Time*. Los Angeles: J.P. Tarcher, 1976.

Volleyball

U.S. Volleyball Association, 1750 East Boulder, Colorado Springs, CO 80909–5766.

Water Skiing

The American Water Ski Association, P.O. Box 191, Winter Haven, FL 33882.

Index

U
United States Auto Club (USAC),
    93
Upshaw, Gene, 80

V
Van Brocklin, Norm, 9
volleyball, 100
Voss, Brian, 89

W
Walsh, Bill, 5, 117, 119

Walton, Bill, 72
water skiing, 100
Watson, Tom, 49–50
Weber, Pete, 4, 89
weight, 19, 80, 83, 90
    training, 29
Wilcox, Rhonda, 5
Woosnam, Ian, 4, 84
wrestling, 19, 20, 65, 97

Y
Young, Steve, 4, 80